Don't Do It Like They Did It – in Washington!

Stop outsourcing of jobs!

Stop inequality of wages!

Stop climate change! No War!

Howard M Greenebaum

DEDICATION

Dedicated to my darling wife, Hilary, who has contributed so much to make these the best 25 years of my life. I hope I can reciprocate as much to you in the next 25.

CONTENTS

ACKNOWLEDGMENTS

I wish to thank my many teachers who have devoted their lives to opening the minds of students to the marvels of the world of learning.

NOTE TO THE READER

This is a book about the decline of a former great democracy. I have written it so you can gather people who value democracy and teach them how to avoid the mistakes we made in America.

For those of you readers who live around the world, and are unhappy with your governments, I have included many ideas to help you build new and better governments.

I am an 82 year old American who has tried very hard to defend our democracy. I ran for public office several times, butting heads against a system that favored money over principle. I wrote a book about campaign finance reform, and lectured at universities all over the USA. I was the guest on 210 radio talk shows explaining the cause and effects of allowing outside interests to fund our elections. I marched and spoke at many anti-war demonstrations in America. I worked very hard to protect the American environment from polluting corporations. I appeared and spoke at many public hearings, trying to achieve just and fair decisions from a flawed government. I wrote many letters to editors of newspapers around the USA.

I love the America that I was born in, and spent so many years enjoying the freedoms of a democracy. Unfortunately, as the years ticked away my country lost its way.

In the years of the 2000s, my country became mired in unjustified wars, and allowed her banking community to cause a worldwide financial crisis, caused by an American government's weakened regulations, and bribed governmental representatives.

Millions of Americans have lost their lifetime savings, their jobs, and their homes. American education has become a victim of the ill chosen priorities of a broken government, which has cut funding for schools while cutting the taxes of the rich.

My wife and I made a very hard decision to leave our beloved country and move many thousands of miles away, to the tiny nation of New Zealand. I have been a long time fan of the New Zealand government, which stood up to America, and refused to allow nuclear powered or nuclear armed vessels to enter their ports.

I have shed many tears over the suffering of our friends and family members, struggling back in the States. This should never have happened. I hope you Readers from other countries will communicate the lessons you have absorbed in this book to your fellow citizens, so it does not happen in your country.

And I hope that many Americans read this book and learn the causes of their misery, and get angry enough to fix their government. On August 18 – August 22, 2011, the Associated Press-GfK poll found that 87% of the polled voters "totally disapprove" of the way Congress is handling its job! So you have plenty of company to help fix our broken government.

There is no problem that cannot be solved if people use their intellects. America can be a democracy again, when the citizens fix the causes of its decline. I hope you fellow Americans learn enough from my book to do the job. For the sake of my family and friends, please do it soon.

Howard Greenebaum
American citizen, Author, and tough old guy

TODAY'S WORLD ECONOMICS SERVES A FEW-AT THE COST OF MANY

Foreign factory workers' lament:
"Sweat! Smoke! Noise! Tired!
How many more hours
before I go home?"

American factory workers' lament:
"Sweat! Smoke! Noise! Tired!
How many more weeks
before I lose my home?"

The Story of Ricardo and Richard

Please visualize- two working men facing each other. Then envision an imaginary national border line snaking between their worn shoes.

On the left side of the border line is a Mexican worker who is employed by X Car Manufacturing Corporation. His name is Ricardo. Ricardo has a wife and two children. He is an excellent mechanic and works very hard. He is paid $3 per hour.

On the right side of the border line is an American worker who also is employed by X Car Manufacturing Corporation. His name is Richard. Richard has a wife and two children. He is an excellent mechanic and works very hard, too. He is paid $21 per hour.

Both men do exactly the same work for X Car Manufacturing Corporation. Why then is Ricardo paid 7 times less than Richard?

The simple answer is that X Car Manufacturing Corporation "can get away with it."

Does the Mexican government know that Ricardo is getting ripped off? Of course they do. Do they care? Or are they bribed to look the other way? You choose, but remember this has been going on for a long time, and there are a lot of Ricardos being ripped off –around the world. (The minimum wage set by the Mexican government in 2010 was a whopping 60 cents per hour!)

Now, there is another part of this story. The X Car Manufacturing Corporation is not happy about this situation. Are they feeling sorry for Ricardo and his starving wages? I don't think so.

How American politics got dirty

The first thing X Car Manufacturing Corporation does is call a meeting of all of their lobbyists. What is a lobbyist? A lobbyist is a well dressed person who is paid a lot of money by corporations to give a lot of money to our elected representatives. These gifts of money are called political contributions.

In 1998 ex-US Congressman Cecil Heftel wrote a book called "End Legalized Bribery." Cecil described political contributions as "legalized bribes." And that is what they are! In the USA, hundreds of millions of dollars are given to candidates in elections and to already elected officials to buy their votes.

The selling of votes is a long hidden secret in the USA. If we counted all of the bribes being given, you could rightly label the USA as the most corrupt nation in the world. Why? Because no other country's bribes can come close to the total of bribes paid in the USA. In 2008 Barack Obama received over $ 700 million in so called contributions to his campaign for US President! Did these contributions affect Obama's decision making?

The US Constitution states that bribery is a felony. (which is a very serious crime). The dictionary defines a bribe as "the receipt of something of value by a person in a situation of public trust, and this person's actions are then influenced by the acceptance of this gift." I wrote a book about this rampant bribery in US elections 8 years before the ex-Congressman's book. Mine was called "Free Elections???" The cover of the book depicted an American flag with a hole in it, and $100 dollar bills flowing through the hole! Today, we would need to substitute one million dollar bills on that book cover!

What happened to Richard, and a few million of his friends?

Let's get back to X Car Manufacturing Corporation and all of their lobbyists. These lobbyists were paid lots of money to visit the elected officials in the US government and bribe them to change the laws. And since nobody in the US government gave the money back, here is what happened to Richard, the guy making $21 per hour. Richard was fired! And so were millions of other hard working Americans! And X Car Manufacturing Corporation moved lots of their car factories across the border, seeking more Ricardos to pay starvation wages.

And how did the US Presidents react to all of the Richards who lost their jobs? They made lots of speeches, and then invited the lobbyists from X Car Manufacturing Corporation to come pay a visit. Then they signed laws that cut tax rates for building the foreign car factories, and gave tax loopholes to move car factories out of the country, and best of all, rewarded them with subsidies for outsourcing millions of American jobs to poorly paid workers all over the world.

That is called redistribution of wealth. Only the poorly paid workers in the other countries did not get wealthy. Some people did get very wealthy with this neat scheme to kill the jobs of American workers. These people are called CEOs. CEOs of many US corporations watched the CEOs of car factories get rich, and they copied these tactics down to the very "t." As the stock prices of these American companies went up from the cuts in wages of millions of Americans, the CEOs' stock options get more and more valuable.

American CEOs are the highest paid executives in the world! Their annual wages are in the millions of dollars. These same CEOs are often seen at public events sporting in the lapels of their expensive jackets, a small American flag suggesting that they are patriots. Is it not time to call them what they really are? Not patriots. Patriots do not fire millions of workers, and plunge their families into poverty. No I think a better name is Traitors.

This is only the beginning of how the United States of America has tumbled from the top of the world towards the basement. And this is why you and citizens in other countries should read this book and learn what NOT TO DO, if you want your country to be free of collusion between corporations and your elected officials.

The sleeping giant

You see voting is not the whole answer to being free. Americans vote all the time, and they think that is all they have to do. After each US election, 99% of the voters go back to sleep until the next election, which is years after their great act of patriotism. Yes, I am being critical of my fellow Americans. Because, their lack of attention to the behavior of their elected representatives is one of the major reasons why America has become the capitol of world governmental corruption.

I wrote a letter in January 2008 to the Chairwoman of the Colorado state Democratic Party, suggesting that the Party create a process called, "Elect and Direct." By that I recommended that the Democratic Party monitor the decisions of our elected representatives, and congratulate them on votes favorable to the general public, and chastise them on votes sold to Special Interests. It is now 2011, and I am still waiting for an answer to my letter. Sometime in 2010 that Chairwoman resigned her position. Perhaps, the new Chair person will answer my letter in 2012.

And American letter writing to their governmental officials is worth some attention. For decades, American citizens have been urged to write a letter to their Congress person with their suggestions to better our country. I, personally, wrote lots of letters. Unfortunately, all that we receive back are form letters with some phony spin talk attached. It is assumed that our officials are too busy to personally write to all the voters.

The truth is quite simple. When most Congress people or their aides look at letters, they hold the letters up to a bright light to determine if there is a check in the envelope. You now know why most of us get form letters. We didn't send money!

What do Congressmen and Senators do in their offices?

Congress people are only elected for 2 year terms. So, they basically spend most of their working time fundraising for their next elections. Because they become such excellent hustlers of political contributions, their average number of years in office surpasses that of US Senators who have 6 year terms. Is this a good system? Of course not. A later chapter in this book will offer a better process for your country to fund elections, and eliminate bribery.

And don't for a minute assume US Senators are more honest because they have such long terms of office. They are not. The Senators have to raise much more money because while a Congress person only represents a fraction of the voters in his/her state, the two US Senators for each US state represent the whole state. They must raise many, many millions of dollars to keep winning elections. Is this what you want "your representative" doing during his/her work day?

Barack Obama

Does this problem include the US President Barack Obama? Yes and here is one example. Before Obama became President, he made lots of speeches about stopping the proliferation of nuclear weapons. In June 2011 Obama's administration began considering spending $ 213 billion "modernizing" nuclear weapons and their delivery systems. This modernization includes making drones capable of carrying bombs! I have not read a word about Obama opposing the terrible direction this is leading the USA.

And this is not all the money the US government is spending on nuclear weapons. They spend $ 54 billion per year on maintenance of nuclear weapons! This adds up to $ 267 billion that can be wasted in one year. Small wonder that the US national debt is rising and spending on education is declining.

And in case you have not noticed, President Obama has been pushing Congress to spend several billion dollars more to build more nuclear power plants in the USA. Meanwhile, Germany, Japan, Switzerland, and other nations have decided to get rid of all of their nuclear power plants. Does anyone not suspect that Obama is hustling campaign donations from the nuclear arms and nuclear power interests?

This is the same President who entertained health insurance lobbyists before the so called health reform law was voted on. And later we find that he opposed the only measure that would have helped Americans afford to buy health insurance - Medicare for All.

This is the same President who signed the credit card reform bill that had no ceiling on interest rates that the banks could charge! And the banks are now charging 30% interest and more to struggling Americans.

A US President does not have to sign laws that a crooked Congress passes. He can veto them. But Obama has chosen to join the bribed Congress and smilingly signed the bills. In Obama's first campaign for President, he raised over $ 700 million! He is heavily obligated to the big corporations who helped elect him.

Money talks

The funding of US elections by corporations and rich individuals is directly responsible for the unbalanced economy of the USA. Bribes have distorted the US tax system, so that many corporations pay no tax, and rich individuals now have tax rates so low that they can accumulate billions of dollars in assets.

Campaigning for re-elections takes lots of money and energy in the US system of elections. These so called representatives of the people spend a whole lot of time "talking" to lobbyists. There are thousands of lobbyists walking the halls of American city, state, and federal offices. The lobbyists continue to visit "our" representatives long after they are elected with their bosses' money. Why are they still visiting? Because their bosses send them there to obtain tax cuts, tax loopholes, subsidies, tariffs on competing foreign products, etc. And that's not all the employers of the lobbyists are interested in.

Climate Change

Most of the manufacturers are very interested in Climate Change, but not for the reasons you and I are. Their lobbyists are there to bribe our reps to vote AGAINST ANY TYPE OF REGULATION that will prevent them from continuing to dirty our air and water. They prefer to DUMP CHEAP.

Many of these same "nice guys" also bribe certain scientists to speak out against the very science that has proven that Climate Change is not only a threat to Mankind, but is already happening in front of our very eyes – with more and more severe storms, floods, droughts, and other so called "natural disasters." Corporations around the world are poisoning our air and water, and causing severe havoc with our fragile planet. And the governments of your country and mine are doing nothing to stop this criminal behavior.

Bribery works. It is working in the USA. And it is working in other countries as well. Is your country free of corruption? How do you know? Is there transparency that enables you to see how your officials get elected? We shall go into all of this as this sorry story unfolds.

Fixing the world's food system

But, let's go back to the world economies. In May of 2011 a story hit the newspapers describing the mass of suicides being committed by poor farmers in India. Since the year 1998, over 100,000 people have killed themselves each year in this one poor country. Approximately 60% are male and 40% female. Suicide occurs when people can see no escape from their suffering. The suffering can be from their health conditions, their poverty, or from various emotional disorders. India has a very large population of poor farmers. They have been crushed by the coming of Globalization, which has removed governmental subsidies and opened the India market to worldwide competition. Is capitalism working when masses of people are losing their ability to survive?

On June 1, 2011 International Oxfam announced the release of a study about how the world food economy is broken and why. Oxfam is an international confederation of organizations working in 98 nations to eliminate poverty and injustice. They not only list the problems, but also the culprits responsible for the suffering, and offer well thought out solutions. I shall condense these findings with a few suggestions of mine. (Oxfam's report is entitled, "Growing a better future" and can be found in its entirety in www.oxfam.org/grow)

Oxfam's report disclosed that only $57 billion has been spent in the world on subsidies for renewable energy, while the fossil fuel corporations have been given $ 312 billion! This is in conflict with all of the scientific studies that have been warning the world of the terrible threats from Climate Change.

There are many contributory factors responsible for the world's imbalanced food economy. One is the speculation on commodities markets. This is supposed to be a tool where corporations can buy commodities at prices that may protect them against future inflation. However, as all such financial markets operate, manipulation of prices can and does happen. This results in inflated prices of much needed commodities, and the obstruction of a true balanced market of supply and demand. These unjustified inflated prices cause great suffering around the world. One such result is poor people devoting 80% of their wages toward purchasing food! My recommendations are to close all commodities markets – or place very tough regulations on these markets, banning speculation. Limiting investments might be one way to keep speculators from pushing prices skyward.

There is another major cause of this broken food system. The system is controlled by three ultra rich corporations. Cargill, ADM, and Bunge control 90% of grain trading! Once more we face the ugly face of huge corporations dominating a market and becoming richer and richer at the expense of the rest of the world. I certainly recommend the breaking up of these giants, so the trading of grain can get back in the hands of the many, instead of the few.

Oxfam's report also found that there is a great need to reduce costs of shipping food. Once more, we should allow more competition, to bring down shipping prices.

Obviously, food production depends on the availability of land and water. The bad news here is that many nations have failed to protect both. Since 1960 the world has lost 48% of its arable land! And by 2030 there will be 30% more demand for water, as the population grows and grows. Water conservation has not been high on the list of building contractors. I recommend that every nation tighten their building regulations for several reasons:

#1 Climate Change is bringing more and more severe storms. So buildings must be built stronger to withstand powerful winds.

#2 Buildings should be built farther from water so they will not be flooded by these severe storms.

#3 Buildings should have two separate water lines. One is for drinking, washing, and cooking. The other line is called, a "gray line." The gray line is for recycling the waste water for uses such as watering gardens, washing cars, etc. We must conserve our water.

Agriculture and our diets need fixing

One of the major problems with agriculture today is the wasteful use of land. 90% of all land is devoted to feeding livestock. Here are the facts: A cow provides a person with only 19.5 kg of protein per acre of land per year, while growing wheat on that same land provides 122kg of protein! Growing wheat is more than 10 times more efficient!

One of the lies about protein is that a human must eat meat to get protein. This is definitely not true. Actually, meat protein is dangerous. The world renowned China Study found that meat protein fuels the growth of cancer, while the eating of a Vegan diet starves the growth of cancer. (The vegan diet consists of grains, fruits, and vegetables. Many of the top athletes in the world exclusively eat the Vegan Diet. The Vegan diet excludes the eating of any type of meat, including not eating fish. It also prohibits eating any dairy, such as eggs, cheese, and milk.)

The easiest way to determine if a food is good for you is to see if a food contains saturated fat. The elimination of saturated fat from your diet is the most important protection from heart disease, diabetes, cancer, and so many other diseases. Never buy any food without looking at the labels! Make sure that your government has a tough agency that checks corporations' labeling to confirm that the numbers are correct and there is no cheating on labels. All foods must be labeled so consumers can ascertain its safety. Also, make sure that your governmental watchdog agency requires large type on labels, so you can read them.

And finally, the quantity of items, such as saturated fat, must be per serving. It is essential that the food safety agency requires standardization of the definition of serving size. Without standardization of serving sizes, each manufacturer can escape safe food standards by varying the serving size. (for ex. one cookie factory says that their quantity of saturated fat is one gram, but states their serving size is one cookie. Another honest cookie factory says that their quantity of saturated fat is 2 grams, but their honest serving size is 6 cookies! This calculates out that if you ate 6 cookies of the dishonest factory you would be eating 6 grams of saturated fat. The crooked factory's cookies actually have tripled the amount of saturated fat in them! Cute trick, but not so funny. The crooked corporation is responsible for the premature deaths of many of their loyal, but uninformed consumers.

For a moment, I would like to pause and focus on the above sentence. I chose the word, "uninformed" not uneducated for an important reason. One does not have to go to university to become informed. Every person who can read is capable of checking the labels on the food that they are consuming. It is the responsibility of all citizens to share this important information about label checking before you buy. You can save lots of people's lives by explaining this bit of information to them. Here is a check list to keep in mind.

#1 Check every label on everything that will go into your mouth!

#2 Check the quantity and the serving size of the following 3 items:

3 Avoid SATURATED FAT

#4 Avoid SODIUM

#5 Avoid SUGAR

#6 COMPARE the amount of these dangerous ingredients in each type of food. The amount will vary by large amounts. (Bring your eye glasses with you when you buy food.)
Another reason for eliminating the use of land to feed livestock is that this wasteful use of land is also dangerous. It contributes 30% of greenhouse

emissions! Yes, it is causing Climate Change! We must change the way we do things- NOW, to save the world, NOT TOMORROW.

Rich countries waste 24% of their food. 51% of people eating the Western diet are overweight! This is the direct cause of heart disease and diabetes, 40% of US grown corn is misdirected into making bio fuel. This is causing the spike in corn prices, and creating a false shortage. Bio fuel should never be made of food. Bio fuel should consist of harvest waste, such as stalks, leaves, weeds, etc. Never food!

The backbone of the world food system is small farms. Many of these small farmers are women. Female farmers are not treated fairly in many nations. They need equal access to technology, resources, credit, and anything else that males get. It is estimated that if they were granted equal access, the crop yields would increase 20-30%. In simple language, they have one arm tied behind their back while males have both hands free! This discrimination of females must end in all nations. Stand up for women's rights. You will be helping your daughters.

Small farms need protection against unfair subsidies given to large corporate farms in rich countries. These subsidies are crushing small farmers all over the world. The core needs of all farmers are arable land, water, access to technology, investment, and credit.

Do not allow the farm land in your country to be lost. We all need land to grow food to live! There will be 2 billion more people in the world in 39 years (2050)!

Why have our governments failed us?

I refer you to this quote from Oxfam, "We must first overcome the vested interests that have paralyzed the political process until now." In my simple words, our so called representatives in our governments have been bribed to protect the interests of a few, at the cost of the many.

As an example, a book entitled," The China Study", was copyrighted in 2006. The information in this book could have saved millions of lives since 2006. Unfortunately, this book has never received the wide spread publicity that it deserves. Most certainly, because it would seriously hurt the many corporations selling bad food to the world. Food with high contents of sugar are bad. Food with high contents of sodium are bad. Food with high contents of saturated fat will kill you early. This news is not good for the media accepting money for advertising bad foods. This news is not good for processed food manufacturers. This news is only good for you. It should be a crime that it has been withheld from you because of collusion between our government officials and the many industries making billions of dollars selling us bad food.

Here is another example of how good food can protect you from bad diseases. A 1999 study by the Physicians Committee for Responsible Medicine and Georgetown University looked at the health benefits of a Vegan diet for people with type 2 diabetes. (There is an epidemic of type 2 diabetes in the world where people eat the Western diet.) One of their studies found that 21of 23 people with type 2 diabetes on oral medications, and 13 of 17 diabetes patients on insulin who ate the Vegan diet for 26 days, were able to stop taking their medicines! During two and three year follow ups, the patients who remained Vegans had retained their gains! Some exercise was also a part of this program.

Why has this remarkable study been kicked under the rug? If you or a member of your family has diabetes 2, wouldn't you have liked to have been informed of this safe and cheap cure from this very dangerous disease? Are we, the public, receiving protection from our government, or are the many industries that profit by selling medicines and bad food being protected? Remember, this study was done in 1999! That is over 11 years ago!

Just imagine if the world had changed to a Vegan diet what would have happened 20 years ago. There would be more land to grow grains, fruits, and vegetables. There would be 30% less air pollution causing Climate Change. There would be far, far less people walking around with pot bellies. There would be far, far less sick people. People who died from these diseases would still be alive today. We would have more money, as eating the Vegan diet is much cheaper than eating expensive meats and dairy.

World economies are stumbling- with the wrong priorities

The crashing of several nations' economies has produced masses of job losses. There is nothing more emotionally disturbing to an individual than losing her/his job, especially when so many companies are not hiring- and you cannot find work. This is happening all over the world. There is something terribly wrong with today's economics. I am an 82 year old businessman who has been a keen observer of the US economy. Since over 50 years of my business years were involved in international commerce, I have also become familiar with other nations' economies. And I have now lived over one year in our new home in New Zealand.

Economies differ from country to country, depending on many factors. The value of a nation's currency has a major effect on its economy. The US dollar has been declining for several years, and now the financial rating of the USA is in the negative, largely due to the exploding multitrillion dollar debt.

While other countries are struggling with multibillion dollar debts, the US government under Barack Obama has adopted a new fiscal slogan, "Here a trillion. There a trillion. Who wants a trillion?" Throwing trillions of dollars at large financial corporations. Throwing trillions of dollars into a war here, a war there, a war anywhere is the modus operandi of today's lost US government. And for those of you who live in other lands, this is a must "not do" lesson to be learned.

The United States of America is mortal. It can bleed and it is not just bleeding, but it is hemorrhaging. Millions of Americans are unemployed. Millions of Americans have lost their homes. Millions of Americans have given up looking for work. Over 51 million Americans have no health insurance. America used to be the country to move to, to get a good job, and live the good life.

America's infrastructure is now ranked 23rd in the world. Studies by the OECD and the World Health Organization found the USA to be 27th in life expectancy, 18th in diabetes, and 1st in obesity! We are ranked # 1 in having the most guns, the most crime among rich countries, and having the most debt in the world. Once more, "don't do what we did."

The Legatum Institute has an index of prosperity that measure material wealth and quality of life for 110 nations. The USA was # 1 in 2007, and has now dropped to # 10. Listed below is the #s 1-9:

Myths about social programs and prosperity

. #1 Norway, #2 Denmark, # 3 Finland, # 4 Australia, # 5 New Zealand, # 6 Sweden, # 7 Canada, # 8 Switzerland, # 9 The Netherlands. #s 1 -9 nations spend more money per capita on social programs, and their people have a better quality of life and are more prosperous. That is a lesson that conservative politicians have yet to learn. They continue to oppose social programs, causing much suffering because of their ignorance or lack of caring. Germany has retained its position as one of the world's most successful exporters, in spite of paying high wages and giving generous benefits to its workers. Once more the USA needs to learn how to do this. Europe has better healthcare than the USA, but spends only half as much money.

Only 10% of the US economy is exports, compared to 50% for Europe. The American CEOs' race to move factories and jobs overseas has destroyed the manufacturing base in the USA. Not smart.

America is not hiring teachers and administrators. They are firing them! In large numbers! The American dream to work in education has now become a nightmare. Our government has their priorities upside down.

Wars are not free

We never seem to see a war that we can't refuse to get involved in. But we have lost our connection to the most important things that should be valued in every country. The US government has elected themselves as "The World's Policeman." I did not vote for that. Did any of You American readers of this book vote to spend your US tax dollars to send your sons and daughters to fight wars all over the world? Just a statistic to remember when debating this subject. The population of the USA is only 5% of the world's population. Why is this tiny 5% fighting wars for the other 95%?

If there are more Hitlers to fight, why should not every nation contribute money and people to stop them? There will be more on this in a later chapter in this book. However, you cannot talk US economics now, and ignore how we spend our US tax dollars. The Soviet Union collapsed largely because of over spending on their military. The retiring US President and former US General Dwight Eisenhower warned the US public to beware of the Military/Industrial Complex. He was so right.

The solution for the United States to fix its economy has many buttons to push. But, certainly, military spending must stop. We cannot afford to fight so many wars. Wars cost lives and cost lots of money. One of the greatest economists in the USA is Joseph Stiglitz. He and Linda Bilmes wrote the book entitled, "The Three Trillion Dollar War". They just concentrated on the costs of the Iraq war, and they estimated that the true costs could be greater than the title of the book. And that's just one war. Their calculations include the huge number of young soldiers returning from war with brain injuries that can cause permanent disabilities. On June 3, 2011 US researchers found that 320,000 military personnel have suffered traumatic brain injuries from the Iraq and Afghanistan wars! Multiply 320,000 times 60 year life expectancies per patient and you have some estimate of the looming costs facing the US government!

Two million US soldiers have been deployed since 2001 into war in the Middle East. Adding to the above bills for brain damage, we must now add the estimated 80,000 veterans who have been afflicted with very serious breathing problems. Several scientists, including some honest ones working in the US government have discovered that these patients have developed post deployment respiratory ailments from dust storms, fine dust containing toxins, and from large dumps burning trash at military bases. Once again, as it was with Agent Orange, the Pentagon and the Veterans Administration have opposed these findings, and are trying to deny the claims.

Wars are not free. They kill and maim many young, good people. They destroy infrastructure. They kill more civilians than soldiers. They are bad. Oh, and they can wreck your economy. There is no way we can separate a discussion of economics and the defense spending of a nation. Many nations spend far too much money on defense. It is time we all spend a whole lot of time figuring cheaper ways to defend ourselves. I will share some ideas on this in later chapters.

War profiteering

Teachers across the whole USA are marching with signs, "No War. Yes Education." They have it right. But once more, let us not forget that army of lobbyists with their check books visiting our elected "reps". There is a lot of money to be made by corporations who sell things to the Pentagon. (The Pentagon is a pentagon shaped building in the US capitol where military leaders sit on chairs and guide our military forces, and order supplies for all of this fighting.) War profiteering is a going business. While our soldiers die, CEOs gather millions of dollars as their companies sell to the US Government.

Wars are crushing our values in many ways, besides the obvious. More on this in later chapters. But in simple words, no country can afford to fight wars indefinitely. The US government has not figured that out yet. Too bad. Remember the slogan: Here a trillion. There a trillion….." (On May 18, 2011 the US Government. announced that the national debt had grown to $ 14 trillion plus $ 294 billion! (the newspapers state 14.2 trillion. I just want you to understand that the ".2" equals $ 294 billion!) And there are some serious doubts about that sum of $ 14.2 trillion. Some respected economists have questioned the methodology used to count national debt. The actual figure may be much larger. It is quite possible that not only do US corporations cook their books, but the US government may also be applying fuzzy math to suit their political needs.

What about Ricardo?

Ok, you say, but what can "you" do for the starving Ricardos? Well, I am glad you are interested in the plight of these severely exploited hard working people. It is my humble opinion that the first thing to do, is to change the "you" to "we". We must all open our hearts to all human beings on this planet, and consider their lives as precious as our own. And I am not asking you to respond to some TV ad that asks you to contribute $9 a month to feed some child in some foreign land. No, I believe that these gestures may make you feel good, but are way off target. What about all of the other children and their parents who are also hungry in this tiny village? Let's take a look at how lopsided is the world economy.

The population in 2011 of the world is 7 billion people.

2.3 billion are well fed.

2.3 billion are under fed

2.3 billion are starving!

1.3 billion people earn less than $1 per day!

3 billion people live on $ 2 per day!

Now that you can see that there are a whole lot of people suffering in the world, let's take a look at who is not suffering.

The world's 1,210 billionaires have assets larger than the annual incomes of more than half of the world. Do you actually know how much is a billion dollars?

A person who has one billion dollars has the same amount as one thousand people with one million dollars each! (simply stated, one thousand millionaires equals one billionaire).

The assets of the world's three (3) richest men are more than the total Gross National Product of ALL the poor countries in the world!

If you are an American reader and believe that all of this does not affect people in America, guess again.

In 1994 the Urban Institute in the US found that 1 of 6 elderly people in the USA are hungry. And this was before; the "so called great recession" occurred and is causing so much havoc with the finances of Americans.

In 1991 in the US, 46% of African American children were hungry. 40% of Latino children were hungry in the US. And 16% of white children in the USA were suffering from hunger.
The USA ranks 23rd among industrialized nations in infant mortality! (This means that 22 other countries have less infant deaths per capita than suffered in the USA.)

One of 8 American children under the age of 12 suffer from hunger.

More than half of all deaths of children in the world are caused by hunger.

So we now have learned that there are poor and hungry people in every nation, including the USA.

Ricardo does not have to be poor!

To understand the causes of this enormity of suffering, we must be willing to open our minds, and try and think beyond what we have been told by the media about economics. And when I say media, I include radio talk show hosts, movies, television, newspaper columnists, etc.

No matter what country you live in, there are people who benefit by the suffering of others. These people are primarily the executives of large corporations who are continuously searching the world for the lowest paid workers. Today's theme for executives is to not only dump cheap (pollute), but to pay cheap (exploit). This results in tremendous losses of good jobs in all industrialized nations, and the continuation of starvation wages in poor countries. It also results in the pollution of the air and water in these poor countries by the invasion of new industries with ruthless management.

This is a race to the bottom. And the final result is well worth considering. If every large corporation continues to fire their workers in their home country and move these jobs to poor countries, who is left to pay taxes for teachers, university professors, policemen, firemen, etc? Who is left to buy products and services? This is now happening in the USA and many, many other industrialized nations. The so called industrialized nations are becoming un-industrialized. They are also becoming poor. And they all are in terrible debt. Corporations are firing the tax payers. They are destroying the finances of their governments and the finances of their consumers. No job. No wages. No buying of products and services.

Why am I repeating this message? Because this gross mismanagement is being practiced all over the world – powered by blind lust for riches. Last year in the USA far more jobs were sent to poor countries than were created in the USA. And the unemployment rate is supposedly 9.1%. But that national figure is not to be trusted. The methodology of counting the unemployed was changed under the presidency of Ronald Reagan, and has never been changed back. The true percentage of unemployment in the USA is probably twice the number, or at least 18%. And far higher in large cities where the minorities, and especially young workers, are stuck in grave poverty, with few places to apply for work. This is what happens when you allow corporations to take control of your governments and escape regulations. Corporations' needs must always be considered behind those of the public, not before.

The rich opposition

But before we consider the solutions to these terrible problems in nations' economies, we must understand that the people who are most benefiting by the present set of circumstances are not going to be comfortable with any changes at all in the way things are going now. They are becoming wealthier and wealthier by the minute. There are more and more millionaires being created. There are more multi millionaires being created. And there are more billionaires being created. And most of these people don't give a hoot about the rest of the world. They just want to be richer and richer. They can never have enough money.

Redistribution of wealth has always been a nightmare of the rich, but they have no qualms with redistributing your wealth into their pockets!

And that is a problem for the rest of us. The wealth in the USA has been moving at a fast and faster pace from the pockets of the dwindling Middle Class into the upper 1% of the population. This 1% hates paying taxes and does everything they can to dodge the tax man. They have been very successful during election time, electing candidates who promise to cut their taxes, destroy unions, and destroy all public programs, including Social Security, Medicare, and Medicaid. This is THE AGENDA OF THE RICH. There is no public program that they would not consider for privatization- so they can make more money – and the public be damned.

Manipulating the masses with lies

Some of these billionaires have been very clever by creating all sorts of good named bad organizations that are deceiving the public. They are paying millions of dollars to spread lies so they can pollute, privatize, and lower the wages of workers. They use these phony organizations to divert the anger of frustrated citizens from their greedy deeds, to other targets. They have been most successful in the USA, by diverting the US public into believing that the cause of all their problems is "big government". Over and over again they plant this slogan into the rich owned media- until most citizens believe that all we have to do is cut the size of the government and everything will be fine.

The facts are rarely considered by angry and propagandized citizens. This is very similar to what Hitler did to divert the German voters from the problems with their economy. He repeated over and over again that it was all the fault of the Jews. That lie cost the lives of millions of Jews, and millions of soldiers during World War II. People can be deceived and it is happening again on a large scale.

We have all been propagandized about economics with the theme that businesses can only make a profit if their employees are paid starvation wages. And many of the elected officials in our nation's governments have been bribed to pass programs that reward corporations to fire local workers and move factories to poor nations. I have seen no discussions in the media about the results of this flawed economic thinking. In most cases, if someone were to suggest that this is not good for the economy, he or she would be called a socialist or communist. Name calling works when your rich friends control the media. There are few vehicles in the USA left to carry the voice of reason. And this is one other very important subject that will be discussed in another chapter of this book.

So, now that I have prepared you for the forth coming propaganda by the rich to try and discourage people from reading this book, I shall offer my ideas on how to not only stop the exploitation of the Ricardos of the world, but how to build a solid foundation for prosperity all over the world. Yes, your country, and all others can become prosperous. The world does not have to have starving and desperately poor people. We can all have full tummies, a decent place to live in, and enjoy stable wages while doing work with value.

Today's prosperity is limited to a small portion of the population of the world. This does not have to be. The USA has the largest consumer market in the world, even though other nations contain far more people. This does not have to be. Many nations have tiny consumer markets and this does not have to be. Students attend business schools and read and memorize the same old ways to do business. This does not have to be. I believe that this happens because one very important element is absent in all of these text books. That element is called ethical conduct; it can also be called thinking morally. It also can be entitled "sanctity of conduct". And it can also be called quite simply being a good man who considers the results of his actions, and how his actions can benefit more of mankind. Does this definition fit the role of today's CEOs?

Unfamiliar thought – Sanctity of Conduct

All of the chapters in this book will contain solutions to this world's problems. However, I would be amiss, if I did not address a solution that will never be offered in any other book of serious thought. The people most responsible for the world's severely unbalanced economies are the leaders of industry, the CEOs. I assume most of these fellas have families. When I was a very little boy, my father used to take me to the movies. Inevitably, I would ask my Dad, "is that man a good man- or a bad man?" Over and over again I would repeat my curiosity about the characters on the movie screen. I suggest that this question should be asked by the children of CEOs to their mothers. "Mommy, is Daddy a good man?" And I also would suggest that the children ask their Daddy "Are you a good man, Daddy?" How many CEOs could be haunted by their children's questions of their personal morality? I believe it is much easier for CEOs to ignore the suffering of the millions of exploited workers, than it might be for these same CEOs to hear their own children question their morality. It is time that we question the psyche of this army of CEOs who can hoard so much wealth, thrust so many people into poverty, and go merrily on their way. Why are we accepting this behavior as acceptable? Why is there so much silence in the media about this atrocious behavior? Poisoning our air and water is not nice, folks. Exploiting millions of people all over the world is nasty. Offering them so little pay that they will go home each day and see their families starving and shivering from the cold is downright BAD! It is time that we all stop accepting this Bad behavior!

At this point, I must assure you that I am not writing this book based on any religious beliefs or any unobtainable goals. I, personally, believe that most people have been denied prosperity because of the greed and ruthless conduct of a very small portion of the world's population, and it is time to put a halt to this unbalanced share of prosperity.

What is a balanced economy?

We all know about the so called "minimum wage". It is misnamed. It should be called the starvation wage. Because people who are only paid the minimum wage are, indeed, hungry every day of their lives. No Mexican on a 60 cent per hour wage can afford to feed himself and his family a proper diet. My recommendation is that the general public wake up and mobilize grand demonstrations for a livable wage that allows every citizen in every country to receive a livable wage. I believe we have the votes. In fact we have an overwhelming majority of the votes to force all governments of the world to pass a standard livable wage for all working people in the world! And I believe that the imaginary line, which I drew at the beginning of this book, which symbolized a nation's border, is erased- and a worldwide livable wage be passed for every worker in every nation. A starter might be $ 2,000. per month which becomes $24,000. per year. You heard me, a worldwide livable wage. The WTO (World Trade Organization) has the power to do this now. We just need to give them a nudge.

Since business operators in poor countries have now fainted from reading this message, let me give you all some advice. These wages do not have to come solely from your pocket. If your nation stops wasting money on military spending, your government could help you phase in this new system with subsidies. And if your government would change their tax system so their nest of millionaires and billionaires pay taxes, there would be a lot more money to help you raise the standard of living in your country, and have a much larger consumer market to sell your goods and services.

There also is another option to secure livable wages. The ILO is short for the "International Labor Organization" which is an agency of the United Nations. This agency stages international conferences on labor standards and labor rights. It is time to push for livable wages. This will be a win/win. Workers will be able to afford to buy more. Businesses will be able to sell more. Let common sense rule- instead of blind greed that only leads to exploitation.

What will be the results of this change? Well, the naysayers will propagandize all types of dramatizations of doom. But the truth will be instant world prosperity! Think about it. For the first time in history, there will be a huge group of consumers in every country with money in their pockets. Businesses will grow at record paces. As people buy, the businesses will have to hire more employees to produce goods and services. More people to distribute. More people to work in retail. More taxes to improve schools, infrastructure, and provide healthcare for all. More construction of homes. This is the reality of a world where fair wages are the standard.

The outsourcing of jobs to poor countries will cease as there will be no more poor people to exploit. Workers can enjoy stability of wages and employment. Governments can enjoy a steady stream of taxes to support social services. And production of products and services will enjoy record growth.

The fears of losses of jobs will be obliterated by the increased classified ads for employment. Our markets will be swamped with buyers. Stores will be ordering more goods to replace the sold items. The local factories will be hiring people to make these sought after products.

All of this will happen because employers in all countries have been forced to pay livable wages. Years ago, Henry Ford, the owner of the Ford Automobile Company, gave raises to all of his employees. Henry's friends asked Henry why he was "over paying" his workers and he replied, "because I need customers to buy my cars." That simple arithmetic still works. If you pay people more money than they need to pay for stables like food and housing, they will buy other products and services. If you pay only starvation wages, they will not be able to buy anything but some cheap food.

Where will the money come from to create these changes?

And so far we have only focused on replacing the minimum wage. If governments have the power to pass minimum wages, why not also pass a law with a maximum wage? Wow! I betcha some rich people just fell out of their chairs with that one. However, let's consider what is happening all over the world because of a lack of a maximum wage. Let's take the USA for an example of "Don't Do It Like We Did." We now have billionaires. These people have literally thousands of millions of dollars. And what do some of these super rich do with their money?

Let's take the two Koch brothers for an example. These two brothers own the second largest private company in the world. Each brother is worth over $ 20 billion! This means the combined wealth of these two men is 40 thousand million dollars! Do they think they have enough? Apparently not, as they are spending millions of dollars trying to deceive the public into believing that there is no such thing as Climate Change. And why are they doing that? Because they own oil, gas, and chemical companies, and they want to keep selling these polluting items and making more billions of dollars.

The Koch brothers are not alone. They hold large meetings with lots of CEOs from other corporations with the same intentions, to bribe our elected officials so they can all become richer, and the people be damned. Their conduct is based on selfishness and greed. These super rich individuals are hoarders of wealth. Their money could buy a lot of food for the hungry millions of people around the world. Their money could have paid the mortgages of millions of Americans who lost their homes to crooked banks and to historic floods, and other severe storms.

The USA now has the most unequal distribution of wealth of any major country! 400 rich Americans own more wealth than 150 million other Americans! The top 1% of Americans now earn more than 50% of what all Americans earn! And this is happening all over the world. The top 1% of the world own 39% of the wealth of the world. And that has increased rapidly from 37% only two years before. There now are 5.2 million millionaires in the USA, 1,530 millionaires in Japan, and 1110 millionaires in China! This terribly unbalanced share of wealth is destroying the world's economies. The largest economy is being damaged the most. As of May 2011, the official unemployment rate in the USA was 9.1 %. However, other more accurate estimates of US unemployment range from 15.8 – 18 %. In US cities, the rate of unemployment of minority races is near 50%. 45% of the US unemployed have been out of work for over 27 weeks. US home prices have declined 33%. American workers are struggling to keep their homes. Foreclosures of mortgages on homes are in the millions.

The city and state governments' budgets are in shambles. These local governments are cutting jobs of teachers, police, firemen, and nurses to balance budgets. Since 2008, over 500,000 people have lost their jobs in these important positions, and the cuts are increasing!

All of this can be fixed fast with a caring government.

The causes of the huge trillion dollar deficits of the USA can be counted on one hand! And here they are:

Tax breaks to rich individuals! Repeal them.

Various tax loopholes, enabling corporations to pay no taxes! Repeal them.

Waging wars! Stop all wars now.

Absence of regulations to protect consumers and the planet! Regulate now.

60% of tax dollars go to military! Declare Neutrality and end era of Militarism.

Unrestrained military spending has not made the world safer. Our intrusions all over the world have made the USA a target for terrorism. Collusion between corporations and our bribed government has resulted in the loss of tough regulations over cheating corporations. Huge financial fraud has started in the USA and spread to other nations.

Bribes have driven down the tax rates of the rich. During World War II the rates for the rich were at 68%. During the 1960s and 1970s the top rate rose to 91%. For most of this long period the rates never were less than 50%. Today, the rates for the rich range from 28% to 35% BUT- special tax breaks for the rich allow them to treat MOST of their income at rates of ONLY 15%!

During this same period of lowering the taxes for the rich, the sales tax and payroll *taxes for the middle class were increased*! When the tax rates were high on the rich, the masses enjoyed great prosperity. Since this has been reversed, the results have been staggering.

In 2001 and 2003 US President George W. Bush signed legislation that gave $2.5 trillion in tax cuts to the rich over a 10 year period. Then, his successor, Barack Obama signed an extension to these tax cuts for the rich for another 2 years! When people elected Obama for President, the voters believed Obama's flowery speeches about "bringing change". It is disgusting to see Obama catering to the rich while the rest of America are suffering. $2.5 trillion could have sent tens of millions of students to college. Instead of today's firing of teachers, firemen, police, and nurses, we could have made our schools better, our hospitals better, and our country safer.

Wake up, America!

We must never be deceived again, by flowery speeches. Americans must stop the bribery and throw out the crooks that pretend to represent the public, but are secretly catering to rich corporations and rich individuals. Enough is enough!

The US law entitled the Glass-Steagall Act was passed during the Great Depression, and separated banks from being both commercial and investment institutions. We, the people, are now in the Second Depression because this vital law was abolished by a corrupt US Congress. It should be reactivated now!

It protected individuals from losing their money by a bank gambling their money on risky investments. Today, banks are once more free from regulation and are busy gambling their depositors' money. This caused the collapse of the US economy in 2008 and contributed to serious losses at banks around the world. Today, the *US banks are spending most of their money in trading and not in lending money to businesses and individuals*!

The CEOs of the largest banks are making an average annual salary of $ 26 million *by gambling on derivatives and other unregulated securities*! All securities should be strictly regulated, especially derivatives, as the derivative market is in the trillions of dollars! The CEOs of the large banks are making twice the salaries of the nonbank Fortune 500 executives. They are highly motivated to continue this risky business of trading in an unregulated industry. The next financial collapse will certainly be related to this gambling, and the *losses will be much larger for the world's economy*! Gambling is addictive. Gamblers always lose in the long run. Unfortunately, the banks are gambling with our money. Not only should this be regulated, but the trades should be heavily taxed, so that investors lose their lust for this so called easy money.

How US financial cheats fleeced the world!

I do believe in capitalism, but I also believe in regulations that protect the public from cheating and hoarding. The so called "super recession" that is still with us since it started in 2008 is a prime example of unregulated cheating and hoarding. American banks, investment companies, mortgage brokers, and real estate companies combined to over sell houses to people who could not afford the monthly mortgage payments. Signatures were forged, incomes were forged, assets were forged, and documents were not required. These worthless mortgages were then bundled into so called securities and bribed financial rating companies gave the so called securities phony high ratings. Billions of dollars were made selling these worthless mortgages around the world. And then came the crash as banks and insurance companies discovered that they did not even know their own worth anymore.

The entire world fell victim to this American made financial catastrophe. Some countries have now set up strict regulations, but many including the USA have only pretended to pass strict regulations. Over a trillion dollars were distributed to these crooked institutions to keep them from collapsing, and a lot of this money went into the pockets of the crooks who perpetrated these heinous crimes making these millionaires richer than ever. The present

Obama Administration has not seen fit to jail any of these crooks. One might wonder if Barack Obama has worried about where his political contributions for reelection might come from if he were to force some of his contributors to be jailed. It is hard to get a pen to write checks when you are in prison. So they say.

The US Government no longer enforces its laws.

In the 1980s another financial crisis was caused by crooked people in the US financial industry. Billions of dollars of savings by individuals were lost to crooked bankers in the US Savings and Loan Institutions. Five US Senators were accused of corruption by their attempts to protect one of the largest perpetrators of these crimes, Charles Keating, who later was sent to jail. And he was not alone. Over 1,000 persons involved in the Savings and Loan Scandals in the USA were incarcerated.

In the 2008 financial crisis that was also caused by crooked people in the US financial industry, only one single person has been incarcerated! And the losses to these crooks were not in the billions, but in the trillions all over the world. US President Barack Obama did not push the US Justice system to enforce US laws. I believe Obama or any other President should never be allowed to pick and choose who is guilty or innocent of any crimes. That is the providence of the Justice system. I believe that Obama is also guilty of not pushing the US justice system to enforce US war crimes laws. I believe that former US President George W. Bush and former Vice President Dick Cheney should have been arrested and charged for war crimes by lying to the public and to Congress about the reasons to attack Iraq. They lied and their lies led to the deaths of hundreds of thousands of people in Iraq, plus the deaths of US military, and deaths of members of other nations' military, involved in this unjustified war. No official should be allowed to exempt people from the enforcement of laws.

This unjustified war destroyed the foundation of the US economy. Crime can only be stopped by enforcement of laws. Many nations have good laws that are not enforced. I caution you readers to demand enforcement of the laws in your country. Non enforcement of environmental laws is causing the deaths of people all over the world. Poisoning of our air and water are criminal offenses.

This description of corporate crime and corporate control of our government by bribes is the result of an absence of strong laws and enforcement of these laws.

Tis the time for a Maximum Wage

A sharp argument for a maximum wage is the need to prevent obscene hoarding of much needed funds for the survival of families. Let's take an example to make the above bunch of words more understandable. A corporation fires American workers and moves the factory to a poor country. The CEO makes over 50 million dollars while the fired workers cannot find jobs. This situation stinks.

Let's paint a different picture. The same corporation does not fire their American workers and the CEO makes only $250,000. The remaining $ 49 plus million goes toward wages for the American workers. Believe it or not, that money can pay for 1,225 workers making $ 40,000. per year. Each million dollars equals 25 jobs at $40,000 per year.

The maximum wage can be made reality by several means. The taxing agency of each nation can tax any excess income over say $ 500,000. by any percentage they choose. There could be taxes on assets, as well, so nobody could assemble assets worth over $ 10 million. That is a nice sum. At 5 % interest you would receive $ 500,000. per year in interests before taxes. Your principal would not be affected, and you could live very comfortably. $ 10 million is still a lot of money.

The wages of CEOs and incomes of all individuals could be limited by taxes to a maximum of $500,000. in income per year. If we limit accumulation of assets and wages, the amount of money paid in taxes to each nation's treasury would surge! There would be no more talk of government debt. There would be plenty of money to develop safe energy and every citizen of the world would be able to escape the pangs of hunger.

In fact with the elimination of hoarding, we all would be well on the way to worldwide prosperity. These are the solid reasons why we citizens must wake up and regain control of our governments. We then can pass laws that favor us instead of rich corporations and rich individuals. This must be done on a worldwide basis so no nation can remain a tax haven where rich people can hide their assets and hide their earnings. Each nation that passes livable wages and maximums on assets and wages can provide prosperity for all of its citizens.

Rich people can be dangerous!

As for the nations with royal families. It is time to count the costs of this fantasy world. The citizens of Great Britain pay over $ 70 million a year to support their royalty. What do they get in return? The kings and princes of the oil producing nations treat themselves royally, but what does their average citizen receive in wages, etc.?

And how many people realize the Saudi Arabian royal family has been funding terrorist groups around the world for years. Remember, 15 of the 19 hijackers who were responsible for the 9-11 bombing of the USA were Saudi citizens. And need we forget, Osama Bin Laden was a Saudi. And a rich Saudi, who financed many terrorist attacks!

In 2011 Saudi Arabia sent mercenaries into the nation of Bahrain to violently put down demonstrations for democracy. Why did the Saudis interfere with protests in another nation? Because they are deathly afraid that their own citizens will throw them out.

And where did the Saudis get the arms to do this? From the same countries who keep saying that they are for democracy all over the world- Great Britain and the USA. Britain has been training the Saudis in public order enforcement and the use of sniper rifles. The USA has been selling billions of dollars worth of military arms and military air planes to these same Saudis who are funding terrorism around the world.

Of course, oil has nothing to do with this total conflict of ideals. And need we forget how the Saudis treat their female citizens.

Our values are upside down

I now would like to address the total picture of wealth, as we see it today through tainted lenses. For a long time every American movie had the leading lady marrying a rich guy at the end of the story. The media still treats rich people differently then you and me. And certainly our elected officials treat them differently, as the "legalized bribes" from rich contributors keeps flowing to them. But there is more than that to think about and question. And this thinking differently and questioning the way things are is exhilarating, isn't it?

Rich people do not have more children than poor people. Quite the opposite. Then why are rich people's houses so big? My father once took a brown and white photo of his father, my grandfather, and had it painted on a large canvas and framed. Why? Because my grandfather, Meyer Greenebaum was a very good man and a very wise man. My father and I greatly admired this gentle man. Meyer once said, "a man can only take a bath in one tub. A man can only sleep in one bed." He said this in context with a discussion of why rich people keep building larger and larger houses for themselves. When I see a mansion, I think they could have saved a lot of money by building a small house and erecting a sign on their lawn that stated, "We are rich!" Same image and lots of less bricks.

My grandfather, Meyer Greenebaum, brought his family over from Germany in the late 1800s. He was a tailor and sold trimmings to other tailors. In 1908 he bought a small diamond ring at an auction and then resold it for $ 50. That was the beginning of Greenebaum's Jewelers, a company that my father managed for 60 years, and I managed for 30 years. When my father died I put the painting of Meyer in one of our jewelry stores, and many times I was approached by customers who told me stories of how Meyer had paid for coal so they could be warm during the Great Depression. In those days, people helped people and did not hire PR firms to publicize their good deeds.

I tell this story because we of the modern world need to get our heroes straight. Athletes play with balls. People like my grandfather helped others. Teachers are my heroes. They choose a job that does not pay much, and they continue to help young people for the rest of their working lives. Super rich people pretend they are good by contributing a small fraction of their money-in a very loud way. Some people are deceived by their PR propagandists. Polluting corporations use advertising to pretend that they are concerned with the environment. It is all smoke and mirrors. When corporations pay no taxes, but make zillions of dollars, they are cheating the public-You! Their cheating results in your taxes being raised or teachers of your children being fired!

How one industry has sunk the ship!

Cheating is rampant in the health insurance industry in the USA, and this has resulted in one specific industry choking a nation's economy. Over 50 million Americans have no health insurance! Millions more have insurance policies that have such high deductibles that many of the policy holders are prevented from receiving medical care because they cannot afford to pay the deductibles. The deductibles on many policies are $10,000. or higher! (Insurance policies require you to pay the deductible BEFORE the insurance company pays anything.) And, even if you are able to pay these high deductibles, you are then required to pay a percentage of the next bills, ranging from 20% to higher. This portion of the policy is called "co-insurance." So a person with a $ 10,000 deductible and a 20% co insurance policy facing a hospital bill of $ 50,000 would first have to pay $10,000 plus at least $ 8,000. Co-insurance adding up to $ 18,000.

When this is explained to patients, many decide to forego necessary medical treatments because of the prohibitive costs. As these medical costs have been transferred from the insurance companies to the insured, the profits of health insurance companies has skyrocketed! And, in spite of these growing profits, the health insurance companies continue to increase their premiums by very large percentages. This price gouging of Americans has forced many families into bankruptcies. Medical costs are the largest cause of personal bankruptcies in the USA.

And this ruthless industry cheats too!

And there is another very nasty side of the US private health insurance industry that also needs to be exposed. Some of the largest health insurance companies have been found guilty of fraudulently refusing to pay legitimate claims. Some companies have employed all types of false statements about their liabilities, in order to escape paying the costs of medical treatments of very sick patients. These denials of legitimate claims have resulted in millions of dollars in profits for these corporations.

Another major blow to the US economy by the private healthcare industry comes from overbilling by private hospital corporations and from overbilling by individual providers. In 1997 the largest corporation operating hospitals was fined $ 1.7 billion for defrauding the US Government out of billions of dollars by overbilling! These fraudulent billing practices were aimed at the two federal agencies caring for the poor (Medicaid) and the elderly (Medicare).

Conservatives in US politics frequently attack these public programs, and have made several efforts to privatize them; always claiming that private management is superior to public. My advice to you, the readers from other nations, is to always be cautious of such propaganda. The CEO of the hospital chain that was fined $ 1.7 billion is a man named Rick Scott. The management of the chain fired Mr. Rick Scott, but in a very peculiar way. They gave him a $10 million severance package, plus stock shares worth $ 300 million, and rewarded him with a $ 1 million per year consulting contract.

Mr. Scott claimed that he knew nothing of these multibillion dollar thefts from the US government, and was never charged. However, two Whistleblowers claimed that the corporation had two different sets of accounting books, and that as the CEO of the whole corporation, Scott had to know.

In November, 2010 this same Rick Scott ran for governor of the state of Florida and spent $ 73 million of his own money to win the election. Since becoming Governor of Florida, Rich Scott has been pushing for legislation to privatize Medicaid and privatize schools! After only 2 months in office, some citizens have begun an effort to recall Scott from his job as governor. Once more the voters in a US election have shown their indifference to details about candidates. Many voters refuse to vote for any candidate who is not a member of their political party. This is like handing a stranger a blank check from your check book. Not smart.

To Be or Not To Be – that is not the question.

Let's pause for a moment and ponder this growing list of problems facing citizens interested in securing a government for their country that will protect the public. Don't forget that the proposed solutions in this book can work in any nation. There is a schedule of how you can create a balanced economy and achieve world prosperity.

First, you the readers must share this information with others. The more people that learn this information, the better chance for success. Distribution of ideas that can help all is everyone's responsibility.

Anticipate opposition, and prepare debate facts

There will always be opposition to any new idea. Especially, these ideas of sharing versus today's minority who cherish hoarding. We must be prepared for threats. The CEOs will pay propagandists in the Media to spread lies that "millions of jobs will be lost." Your answers must be ready to confront each effort at deceit. The obvious answer here is how come the world's largest economy can afford to pay good wages while our poor economy only pays starvation wages?

And if you live in America, and the same bull is thrown around, your answer is, "Since you CEOs have been shipping our jobs out of the country, our own economy has taken a nose dive that is accelerating. If the wages of workers in other nations are raised, you have no more reasons to keep firing my friends. Your ruthless tactics have destroyed the finances of millions of Americans. Why should we trust you?"

If CEOs of corporations threaten to move their whole corporation to another nation, you might remind them that your government can then place tariffs on their products and severely impact their future sales.

There are many arguments that you can use to win the debate for Livable wages. First, you need facts. Is the local company owned by a foreign company? How much were their sales and profits last year? How much did the CEO of the owner company make in wages last year?

Mobilized millions cannot be defeated

As the ideas of this book become popular with the public, the next stage of action is to mobilize. People must meet and from the beginning, create an email list and other internet lists from social networks. As the excitement grows, the internet must be utilized to call meetings and organize a political party with candidates that you can trust. There must be a list of goals that are publicized so they become real to everyone.

Public demonstrations must be carefully organized with the theme of non-violence stressed. Violence must always be avoided. You can organize strikes, work stoppages, but no violence at any level. This is called civil disobedience. This will be in contrast to the tactics employed by the opposition. But, if Mahatma Gandhi could win independence for India, why can't any other group of good people achieve the same by non-violence. The main thrust of any worthwhile public movement must be to win the minds of others. If the numbers grow and grow, there will be no way to stop the long needed changes in your economy.

Advice for the rich

For those rich readers of this book, will this shrinkage of your wealth be so bad? I wonder. I suggest that you may be surprised. I suspect that most zillionaires suffer from guilt. You, deep inside, know that you have been acting badly. You will never be able to totally shield your eyes from seeing the suffering of others because you are hoarding wealth that could be helping others escape from despair. Yes, you are guilty. You have been deceived by a culture of selfishness and insensitivity to others. Yes, you have way too much money hidden from the tax man.

Think of how different your life can be if you have a maximum of assets of $ 10 million. You don't have to compete with your friends anymore. You might even consider living in a non- gated community and befriending people of less wealth. Your children might have to get jobs and work! You might even feel a very heavy weight being lifted off your shoulders.

Since you do have quite a good mind, you might want to use it to accomplish good things instead of solely focusing on getting yourself richer and richer. You might suddenly wake up and feel good about yourself. You might try hiring instead of firing in the workplace. You might make efforts to clean up the waste from your factories voluntarily, and actually desire to protect others from being harmed by pollution from your company.

You might even join the growing army of world citizens who will be working for a world of prosperity for all, peace for all, and protection of our planet from pollution. And, of course, You might sit down and realize that you and your family can live quite comfortably on assets of $ 10 million, and an income of $500,000.00 per year.

Get out of the box – coordinate with like thinkers in all nations

Ok, so much for helping out the rich readers of this book. Let's get back to you, the other 99% of the world.

I strongly recommend that the people of your nation coordinate your activities with the people of neighboring countries. This coordination will destroy the propaganda by the opposition that the employers in your country will simply move their factories and jobs across the border. All people must work together to stop the exploitation of so many by so few. Do not rush into action. Expand and expand. Help neighboring nations organize. Share your ideas with them. The bottom line is that if all workers are paid livable wages, there will be no more hoarding by billionaires, and people in every nation will be able to spend more money which will build industry in every nation.

Simplify your messages, so all people get it

To American readers, you need to publicize this slogan, "Let's stop the race to the bottom!" When all good American jobs have been sent to poor countries, what is left for me and my children in America? We want a "race to the top!" where all workers are paid livable wages, and corporations stop exploitation of workers in America and out of America. Enough is enough. Show compassion for workers in all nations. This brotherhood of workers cannot be broken down by phony propaganda. Create your own means of communication by the Internet so the truth can be shared and propaganda confronted with truths and facts.

Economics is an interesting subject when it is broken down into simple parts. I have endeavored to deliver the messages of this book in simple parts. This book has not been written for a select few intellectuals. I have endeavored to reach the minds of the many workers in the world who are now being paid starvation wages. I want these people to find hope in my book. I want these people to learn that they deserve far higher wages than they are now receiving. I want these people to learn how to join together and share in the prosperity of the world.

Hoarding hurts us all

No one person should be allowed to hoard wealth at the cost of so much to others. Hoarding is criminal because this conduct results in great harm to others. For every one million dollars hoarded- 25 jobs of $40,000 are lost! Let's take a look at how hoarding affects lots of jobs. There are quite a few people who today have hoarded at least 100 million dollars. 100 million dollars of hoarding equates to 2,500 jobs paying $ 40,000 per year! Now let's look at the 1,210 billionaires. One billion dollars of hoarding equals 25,000 jobs paying $40,000 per year! Since there are 1,210 billionaires in the world in 2011, their combined hoarding equals over 30 million jobs! But this number is very low because many of these billionaires have far more than one billion dollars.

Remember Ricardo who works in Mexico? The richest man in the world is Carlos Slim. And he lives in Mexico! Mr. Slim has hoarded $ 74 billion. His assets equals 1.9 million jobs at $40,000 per year. Since we are using a person's assets, we must recognize that many of the 1,200 billionaires have far more than one billion dollars. So the combined assets of just the 1,210 billionaires can pay for many years at $ 40,000.

And we have not even begun to count all of the multi millionaires who are lusting to join the billionaire list. After all, how can a person possibly get by with only 100 or so million dollars! Needless to say, hoarding is costing the world a huge chunk of potential prosperity. And that is what this book is trying to explain.

Unbalanced economies are caused by greed and cheating

The structure of today's economies is wrong. Very wrong. It is awful. It is hurting billions of innocent people. It is causing suffering to so many because it is very unbalanced, very unfair- and it needs to be changed by you the readers. There is plenty of wealth to provide plenty of jobs and pay for food, shelter, and lots more. We just have to stop people from hoarding.

When we were all children, how many times did your mother or father tell you to share? At what age did we forget that lesson? At what age did we decide that we should hoard as much as we can and the Hell with everybody else. That is why so many ultra rich people hire PR companies to publicize their so called giving. They are afraid that you may someday wake up and say, "Enough. You must stop hoarding!"

How did this happen? How did so many people become so selfish and greedy? What happened to their morality? How did they become so focused on themselves that they have become lost in a fantasy world. These same people live in gated communities. Their lifestyles have isolated their consciousness from the real world. They cannot see what their hoarding is doing to the rest of us. They have lost the ability to empathize with others. Their world is small and insensitive.

Hoarding is a threat to humanity

Many of the ultra rich use their wealth to buy hundreds of thousands of acres of land. Once this land is owned, it is under the control of these rich and selfish individuals. Is this sensible or safe for the rest of us? Other ultra rich people use their wealth to change our laws so they pay little or no taxes, and our taxes are raised as a result. Is this the way a democracy is supposed to operate?

Other ultra rich people are using their wealth to change the educational systems in their countries. Can we trust these same selfish people who think nothing of firing thousands of their workers, to change our schools? Is this the way a democracy is supposed to operate? Hoarding produces many bad things on the rest of us. We lose control of our land, our schools, and our way of life. Hoarding must be exposed as the root of much evil being foisted upon us.

Learn how to defend these changes

At this junction, once more we must prepare to defend these new thoughts we are having about creating a balanced economy which will prohibit hoarding of wealth. This does not mean that we do not believe in working hard and smart, and accumulating some wealth. We are not against entrepreneurialism. We just believe that we all must combine our working goals with a sense of morality. By that I mean, we need to acquire a perspective of what is reasonable wealth that does not impact negatively on the rest of us.

Gaining a small amount of millions of dollars, such as 10 million is not going to hurt anyone. But allowing ourselves to grope for more and more wealth at the expense of others is vulgar. And it does hurt many, many people in all parts of the world. People go hungry because of hoarding. People lose their homes to crooked banks because of the ugly tentacles of hoarding corporations. The growth of some corporations is at the cost of the losses of many jobs. Some corporations are good and some are real bad.

We must control corporations, not the reverse.

We should not allow corporations to grow so big, that they are labeled " too big to fail." In other words, no matter how poorly they have treated their customers, they have been given billions of our tax dollars to keep them from going bankrupt. I believe that the antitrust laws in the USA have not been enforced properly and bribery has raised its ugly head again. I believe that every nation should restrain the growth of corporations to a level where competition does not get stifled. And that a corporation is not allowed to grow so large that its failure could cause havoc to others. We have allowed this to happen in the USA and it is wrong. Do not allow this to happen in your country.

Americans must work to get their antitrust laws strengthened and enforced. American voters must elect candidates who support regulations that protect the public from bad corporate behaviour. Unfortunately, there is an epidemic of this today in the USA! I shall discuss this subject in detail in another chapter of this book.

Our value system must be revamped

I recently read a book about Albert Schweitzer. He was one of history's most gifted humans. With all of his gifts, he decided to become a doctor and move to Africa and save poor people from suffering from diseases. This doctor could have become very rich by remaining in Europe and serving the rich. He was a world renowned musician, theologist, philosopher, and distinguished medical doctor. He lived among the very rich. They were his patrons. When he decided to move to Africa, his friends could not understand why he was going. But I believe you readers can understand Albert Schweitzer's reasoning. This was a real hero. He was a man's man. He chose to help others over himself. His story is very worth reading. He was born in 1875 and died in 1965 at the ripe old age of 90. Albert believed that his book that I read was his most important book. He wrote it while he served the poor in Africa. The title is "Out of My Life and Thought," published by The Johns Hopkins University Press. I found it in a small library in New Zealand. This is a quote from this great man's book, "Two observations have cast their shadows over my life. One is the realization that the world is inexplicably mysterious and full of suffering. The other that I have been born in a period of spiritual decline for mankind."

It is nice to pause and think of such a good man, and how one person can do so much for others. Sanctity of conduct must be at the top of any list of values we all should aspire toward. Accumulation of wealth should be at the bottom.

Corporate tax cheating affects everyone

So, back to the subject of hoarding, but with a different set of perpetrators: I want you all to learn how to keep large corporations from impacting your economy negatively. No nation's economy can survive without taxation. Every industrialized nation has developed a fast flowing infrastructure, so goods can be moved quickly. Taxes paid for the building of this infrastructure, and taxes continue to pay for the maintenance of this large infrastructure.

Every industrialized nation has a large payroll of workers who supply safety (police and firemen), sanitation, and education (teachers). Taxes pay these valuable public servants' wages. Although nobody likes to pay taxes, most of us do and understand why.

However, in the USA large corporations are unique. At one time US corporations actually paid their share of taxes. At first glance at the tax rates of corporations in the USA, you would question the above statement, because the actual tax rates are similar to other nations, and higher than many. Unfortunately, the actual taxes paid are quite different in the USA. The US Government Accountability Office found that 55% of US companies paid zero taxes for at least one year in the last 7 years. Their lobbyists have done a great job of bribing our so called representatives. They succeeded in getting their bribed Congressmen and Senators to inject various tax loopholes, tax breaks, and exemptions so that their client corporations totally escaped paying any taxes.

Some corporations actually succeeded in getting subsidies paid to them in years when they were making huge profits! The best example of that are the oil and gas companies who are enjoying huge profits, in the billions, and still receiving subsidies from our tax dollars!

The lobbyists have also succeeded in getting special laws passed that allow US corporations to escape paying taxes by keeping the profits overseas. Another tax dodge is by locating their so called "headquarters" across the US borders. These are called tax shelters. The US government collects about half as much of Gross National Product as do other nations' governments from their corporations. Bribes work! Most nations collect about 2.5 % of output. The US only receives 1.3% of output in taxes from US corporations!

With all of the above tax toys corporations have received, they are still not satisfied. They have also been allowed by a bribed government to employ "creative accounting practices." Another description of this behavior by their accountants is called, "cooking the books." In simple words, it means lying about the expenses and revenue. Estimates of taxes lost by these distorted numbers range to over $ 50 billion! And that may be a low number.
So, my advice to you readers from other nations is to create a tough regulatory agency which will have the power to send crooked corporate accountants and crooked CEOs to jail.

And to create another tough investigative agency to monitor the finances of every elected member of your government. This agency must have the power to send any elected officials to jail if they are proven to accept any bribes. Bribery is the cancer of government. Elections must be funded by your governments, with a total ban on outside participation. "No bribes allowed in my country!" must be not only stated, but backed by tough actions. Bribery is a crime.

Austerity is not the answer to solving a government's debt problems

As this book is being written in 2011, citizen demonstrations are occurring all over the world, as people are angry at their governments for trying to balance their budgets on the backs of the middle class and the poor. The public is becoming aware of the ways that their governments are favoring the rich by cutting public programs that provide education, safety, sanitation, etc. to the general public - instead of raising the taxes of the rich. We should always be suspicious when this happens. Are bribes being given by the rich to get such preferred treatment? Why do governments allow people to hoard billions of dollars while the other citizens are suffering?

Changing each nation's economy from an imbalance of wealth to one which allows its citizens to become prosperous should be the goal of every government. A balanced economy will greatly increase the flow of tax dollars from the growth of consumption by the newly created middle class of consumers. The rising wages and surge of taxes from the maximum wage law should chase away the debts of governments. And the cuts in military spending by every nation should also make large contributions toward shrinking the world of nations' debts.

Every government should be free of outside interference

The founders of the US Constitution were very concerned by the impact of outside Special Interests. I suggest that these Special Interests can be divided into 3 categories, and laws passed to erect barriers between these interests and the public interest.

Thomas Jefferson was responsible for the words, "Separation of Church and State." He believed that a government must not allow religious beliefs to interfere with the running of a government which was being created for all type of believers.

I believe that there also should be a strict requirement to create a " Separation of Corporation and State." This law must ban all gifts or contributions of money to pass from any group of people or from individuals to candidates for public office, or to elected officials serving in government. This law must have strong teeth of enforcement so bribery is snuffed out of every nation's government.

And I believe that a third law needs to be passed that states, " Separation of Military and State". The citizen government must have the authority over the military. In other words, the military must serve the government and be prevented from interfering in government. This law must ban military coups and any insubordinate acts by military leaders. Once more this law must have the teeth to enforce a necessary barrier to military takeovers of nations.

All of the above legal measures can assure you that your government will represent your interests and not be able to appease certain Special Interests or certain rich individuals that can result in an imbalanced economy that favors the few over the many.

Citizens of all nations need to ignite discussions about changing our governments' priorities- and our own priorities

Today we, indeed, have imbalanced economies. Too much money is spent on waging wars. Too much money is spent on selling military arms. The USA is not only spending the most money on waging wars, but is also guilty of selling the most military arms to other nations.

Once more we must not only consider the bribery from "defense contractors" that motivates elected officials to vote for war instead of peace-but another factor that allows this type of behaviour. I am referring to the absence of conscience, or simply put, "acting good." How do so many participants allow themselves to be deceived by the glitter of gold? Defense contractors are people. Engineers in defense factories design weapons to kill more people than the current weapons can. They design drones that have no conscience, to drop bombs from the skies on people and kill and maim them. Defense contractor salesmen make large commissions selling arms all over the world, with no concern with the results of their behaviour.

Should riches be valued over other considerations? How big a house do you need? How many houses do you need? How many cars do you need? How many pairs of shoes do you need? Are you in a spending race with your friends? What would you really like to do every working day? Why do I bother asking these questions? Well, suppose a lot of people began to ask themselves these questions? We would see more decisions made for the good of others.

Suppose people of ultra wealth suddenly became embarrassed by their possessions? Why shouldn't they? Why have we given them a blank check of endorsement to their excessive spending for needless items? Who crowned the wealthy? Why have no writers in modern times sat back and criticized the silly possessions of the rich? At least wonder how a rich person keeps from getting lost in their huge mansions? At least wonder what they are afraid of with their walled in castles? Is morality a lost subject today? Shan't a person or two pose questions above today's shallow dialogue? I have some suspicions about this, and will dwell on them in later chapters in this book.

But here is a quote from a very wise man who lived from 1895-1983, Buckminster Fuller. He stated, "Let architects sing of aesthetics that bring Rich clients in hordes to their knees. Just give me a home, in a great circle dome where stresses and strains are at ease."

Years ago, I attended a lecture by Buckminster Fuller at Johns Hopkins University in Baltimore, Maryland, USA. His wisdom was so respected that extra rooms besides, the giant auditorium, had to be wired so the crowds of students and citizens could hear his message. I took away from this lecture a central theme that BF was stressing. "We can solve any problem if we use our intellect." (This lecture was given at a time when many people were afraid of the world being destroyed by nuclear bombs.) We now have forgotten about all the nuclear bombs standing around, and are worrying about all the nuclear power plants built by earthquake fault lines!

I believe that Mankind can survive if more and more people use their intellect to address more deeply the problems facing the world today. I believe that the status quo is very dangerous, and if no changes are forthcoming, there will be more and more dangers lurking around the corner. Climate Change is already happening- as one clear example. Selling more and more arms around the world is certainly not a building block for world peace. However, I would like to add that intellect must partner with morality in its efforts.

I once wrote across a picture of Albert Einstein, " the world's dumbest man". I wrote this because Einstein's Theory of Relativity enabled scientists to invent the atomic bomb. I believe if Einstein had thought out how people would use his theory, he might have changed some numbers and prevented the creation of the world's worse invention.

Yes, we are addressing economics in this chapter, but we must also not ignore the other factors that affect the structure of a nation's economy. The USA is directing a much too large part of their financial resources to military spending. How does this get changed? Will the US economy crash if we stop spending so much for our so called "defense". Not necessarily.

A transition from a military dominated budget to a peace budget must be accompanied by smart planning. The factory that is producing tanks can produce automobiles. The scientists, who are employed designing kill machines, could be using their brains to design a national network to carry solar and wind power to all of the cities. The inventors of new military devices could be spending their time inventing batteries that can run electric cars, and inventing nano-technological machines to harness solar energy so each home in the world can be heated from the sun at an affordable price. For much too long military spending has held America's greatest minds in hostage, creating destruction, instead of creating construction.

Military spending produces far less jobs than other industries for the same dollar. Education creates 3 times more jobs than the same money spent on the military. Healthcare produces far more jobs for the same buck. Clean energy produces at least 50% more jobs. In summary, peace industries produce far more jobs than the same money spent on building death machines. Soldiers receive far less pay than civilians. They also are more prone to health problems, and they do not receive as good healthcare as civilians. Militarism is destroying the US economy and is responsible for a large brain drain from peace industries to death industries. We need to redirect our bright minds towards goals that will benefit all peoples, and not just the war profiteers.

You may want to save the following summary for future use

We now may want to take a pause and summarize what we citizens can do to change the economy of our particular country to a balanced economy that will provide prosperity to all instead of today's economy which caters only to a few.

#1 We must share this information with others so they can join us in forming a great, giant movement for change.

#2 We must organize, harnessing the power of the Internet and Social networking programs.

#3 We must simplify our goals so we can attract millions under our flag of truths.

#4 We must demand an International Minimum Wage law be passed that is not a starvation wage, but a Livable Wage. I suggest a minimum of $2,000 per month. The WTO (World Trade Organization) may be the device that we use to pass such legislation.

 #5 We must demand a maximum wage and maximum accumulation of assets law be passed, thereby prohibiting the major cause of imbalanced economies, which is the crime of Hoarding. I suggest that the maximum income be $ 500,000. per year, and the maximum accumulation of assets be $ 10 million. This same law must be passed by all nations so the hoarders can find no nation as a tax shelter to hide their assets.

#6 We must demand changes in our national constitutions so we can stop bribery in our elections and also inside of our governments. All elections should be funded by tax dollars, and there must be a strict law that bans all gifts of value or money being passed to candidates or to elected officials by corporations or by individuals. This includes a ban by an individual to give his or her own money to their campaigns. There should be a government agency created that has investigative powers and enforcement powers that can result in the incarceration of persons found guilty in giving or receiving bribes.

7 We must demand changes in our national constitutions so we can establish a separation of Church and State, a separation of Military and State, and a separation of Corporation and State.

#8 We, citizens, must not only vote, but must continue monitoring the decisions of our elected officials so we can determine if their actions are affecting positively the public interests.

#9 We must demand that corporations pay a fair share of taxes, and that all tax loopholes, exemptions, and tax breaks be repealed. That there be no legal way for a corporation to shift tax liabilities to other countries. And that an agency be created to examine the accounting of each corporation to determine if the expenses and revenue has been counted exactly. This agency should be empowered to examine and enforce the law of disclosure. If unlawful behaviour is discovered, and the persons are found guilty of fraud, they should be incarcerated for public theft.

10 We must demand that all laws be enforced and no public official be allowed to grant pardons or exempt any person from the rule of law.

11 Every nation should create antitrust laws that prevent corporations from growing so large that competition is stifled, and they are considered " too big to fail." Corporations that are " too big to fail" should be split into smaller corporations , so the public is not threatened by their failures.

Some things should be non-profit

A final thought on world economics. I believe that certain services and products should not be on the open market subject to price increases and sold for profits. For example, the prices for nursing home care are out of the reach of most people, as are the prices for nursing home insurance. And the conflict between proper patient care and the profit motives of the owners of nursing homes result in patients losing out. Patients in nursing homes need a great deal of care. Many are bed ridden and are unable to even feed themselves. This extensive care is costly.

My mother was a patient in nursing homes for 14 years. I was the sole person responsible for my mother's care during those 14 years. I noticed the call lights on up and down the halls of the several nursing homes that my mother lived in. The numerous call lights on by the doors of patients mean that each of these patients needs someone to care for their many needs. The more call lights on, the more people in need. It is probably impossible to provide adequate care for all of these needy patients and still make a profit. So, care is sacrificed, so profits can be pocketed. This is wrong and should be addressed immediately. I recommend that the governments of nations provide this care on a non-profit basis. It is the only way that disabled and very old people will ever receive the care that they deserve. By passing a maximum wage on all wages in all countries, the money will be there for this situation and many others.

One of the most profitable industries in the world is the manufacturing of medicines. However, the USA and other nations spend large amounts of tax payers' money for research for the cures of diseases. In many situations, the pharmaceutical companies then use the results of tax payer monies to make and sell these medicines at huge profits. This is wrong and it is hurting a lot of people around the world. The manufacturers get patents on medicines and this prevents competitors from making these medicines and selling them at a lower price. Poor people are not able to afford to buy some high priced medicines and die as the result of this unfair system.

I recommend that patents on medicines be abolished so all manufacturers are allowed to compete in the sales of these life saving products. And I also believe that medical research paid by the government of medicines should not be shared with for profit manufacturers. They did not pay for it and they should not be allowed to profit by it. This research should be directed to non-profit contracting manufacturers who get paid by the government to produce these medicines and distribute them at non-profit prices.

Barack Obama

When US President Obama promoted a so called health reform bill, he did some curious things while the proposed law was being discussed. He welcomed a crowd of lobbyists from the insurance industry into his office and had secret meetings with them.

Later when a public hearing was being conducted by Democrat Senator Max Baucus on this law, another curious thing happened. At this public hearing a group of doctors and nurses attempted to introduce their ideas about how this law should be written. They were not allowed to introduce their ideas, and Security officers were called and they all were forced to leave the so called public hearing. What these doctors and nurses wanted to introduce was a government run plan, similar to ones in other industrialized nations. Because the health insurance companies could not compete with a government run program for all Americans, their lobbyists made a deal with the President of the United States! This deal was not in the interests of American citizens. It was in the interest of Obama and his contributors.

Every American could have been covered by a government run plan and been able to enjoy a very affordable healthcare plan. Since 1965 all Americans aged 65 and older are able to qualify for a government run healthcare program entitled Medicare. Millions are insured by Medicare and are very happy with their government run program. It is a disgrace that Obama and Senator Baucus prevented this from happening. Instead, doctors and nurses were treated like criminals for suggesting such a program for people under the age of 65, and were pushed out of a public hearing at the Capitol of the United States!

We now need to understand what actually is happening here. First US President Obama allows lobbyists to discuss in secret a pending law that affects every Americans' health, and then a US Senator does not allow doctors and nurses to speak about this pending law at a public hearing. The bottom line here is money. Obama needs money to run for reelection. Senator Baucus needs money to run for Senator again. This motivation for campaign money stopped any discussion for a national healthcare program run by the government. This money protected the insurance companies' profits from being challenged by a government run program.

The original Medicare program was up in running in 1965 in only eleven months. The final phony health reform bill had provisions that will not be available to the public for several years!

The current Medicare program has some financial problems because it is not like the national programs in other nations. American Medicare only is available to the most vulnerable consumers- the elderly and the severely disabled. Expanding Medicare to all Americans, would immediately cure its finances because it would then be receiving premiums from millions of people who are healthy and who would not be producing large medical claims.

In addition, Medicare could easily begin coverage for all citizens without any delays that are plaguing the phony health reform bill signed by Obama. You see, by offering Medicare to all citizens, the government could then combine two other huge agencies that already have trained personnel experienced with medical costs. These agencies are the Veterans Administration that covers all the medical expenses of the US military. And the Medicaid Agency that covers the healthcare of the poor.

Incidentally, the current Medicaid agency only covers the very poor, excluding millions of people who are quite unable to buy for profit health insurance. And don't forget the millions of Americans who are now unemployed and do not qualify for any type of healthcare program because they have health pre-conditions that disqualify them. The Medicaid agency is currently under attack by the many state governments who are cutting their budgets on the backs of those extremely poor by severing funds to the Medicaid agency.

Beware of private health insurance plans

So for those of you who can afford private health insurance in other nations, here is a bit of advice from a health insurance expert. Read the details of your private health insurance policy. In most cases you will find that if you have any type of pre condition some policies may have no limit on the time you must disclose this information on your application. If you forget to disclose a pre condition that occurred 20 years ago, and you become ill, you may have your claim denied. In the USA, every state has different laws and regulations pertaining to health insurance. In some states, if you have been clear of cancer for 5 years you do not have to disclose this pre condition. Every nation should require a time limit on disclosure of pre conditions.

Another problem that may loom for those on private health insurance is waiting periods for coverage of pre conditions. In New Zealand, the largest health insurer requires a 3 year waiting period on every serious health problem you have had in the past. This means if you had a heart attack 5 years ago, and you have another while insured, you will not be covered until you have been paying premiums for 3 years! In the USA the waiting period is usually 6 months to one year. That is a big difference when you get sick. I believe that the waiting period should be no longer than one year.

Since the phony reform bill was signed by Obama, the insurance companies have raised their premiums even higher and are enjoying record profits- in the billions of dollars. The continuing increases of premiums is choking the US economy! And thousands of Americans die each year because they have no access to healthcare.

These sad happenings should not be happening. But they are. Isn't it time that the American public recognizes the need for change and gets involved in making these changes. Please tell your friends to read this book and learn how changes can be achieved by ordinary people like you and me.

WHO'S AFRAID OF THE BIG BAD WOLF?

"A plane exploded into the tower
of the world's great Superpower.
President Bush screamed, War! War! War!
Instead of questioning, "Why? Why? Why?"...........H Greenebaum

America spends more money on so called Defense than most of the world, combined. America has over 900 military bases spread all over the world. America also sells more military arms, including military air planes than any other nation in the world to other nations. Does that make sense? The US Congress has elected their military to be the world's policeman. Do any of you American readers remember ever voting to send your children to fight wars all over the world?

The bombing of New York City by 19 hijackers of US planes sent America into a panic. All the wrong questions were asked. And all the wrong answers brought all the wrong actions. 15 of the 19 hijackers were Saudi Arabian citizens. So then why did America invade Iraq? Better yet, why did America invade any country?

Why people become "terrorists"

The hijackers knew that they would die by deliberately crashing these air planes into buildings. They still did it. This was the thinking of desperate men who believed that nothing else could change the foreign policies of the Superpower, the United States of America. The reasons behind their violence dated back to the first Gulf War when the US military built a base on the soil of their country, Saudi Arabia. These men believed that this intrusion was wrong.

The second reason why these men sacrificed their lives was their beliefs that the USA was supporting Israel in their harsh treatment of the Palestinians. They lived near Israel and witnessed the occupation of Arab land by the Israelis. They were furious that the Israelis were allowed to take thousands of homes from the Palestinians and not pay a penny for their properties. They witnessed the building of a wall across the properties of Palestinians by the Israelis, thereby depriving these people of their farm land and means to making a living.

They witnessed the US government vetoing any action by the United Nations that would have begun to right any of these wrongs against the Palestinians.

They witnessed the US government arming the Israeli army, and sending Israel billions of dollars in foreign aid.

They also- and this is the most important reason of all- witnessed the US government totally ignoring the plight of the millions of Palestinians who were forced to live in refugee camps around the Mid-East. They believed that Americans did not care about Palestinians. They believed that America only cared about Israelis. They believed that America's foreign policy for the Middle East was heavily tilted in one direction, and not the least bit balanced. Today, more than 60 years since Palestine was "partitioned", over one third of all Palestinians still live in refugee camps, and there still is no Palestinian state.

In retrospect, do you readers believe that IF the US foreign policy had treated the Israelis and the Palestinians equally that 19 men would have given their lives in plane crashes?

I believe that terrorists are desperate persons who see no solutions. They believe that they must act violently to bring about justice. I do not ever believe that killing innocent people is justified. But I can understand how people can become so disillusioned by injustice that they act desperately. This is why some people steal bread to feed their families. They cannot sit by and watch their family starve to death. This is why some people commit suicide. They see no answers to their desperation.

Flawed foreign policies can backfire

This is why the foreign policy of every nation must treat every other nation with respect and there should be no ganging up on anybody- unless there is another Hitler. This, and only this, I can understand. Nobody should be allowed to kill millions of their fellow mankind.

We, the citizens, must cast aside any efforts to demonize the citizens of another nation. We must all learn how to see beyond our eyes into the minds of others. We should stop believing that the color of a person's skin makes him or her inferior. Mutual respect cannot be under stated. It is the formula for peace and kindness. Prejudice harms others and should never be acceptable. We should never, ever tolerate unkindness to others. Bullying in schools is a signal that this lesson is not being taught correctly there.

It is time to put our thinking caps on

The entire consideration of waging wars must be openly debated by the citizens of every nation. Sending young people in uniforms to kill other young people in uniforms must be exposed as behaviour that is totally insane. Dropping bombs on people's homes would never happen if put to a vote. Who gave the green light to manufacture land mines that eventually end up blowing up children? Why is America still spending billions of dollars to develop more advanced weapons to kill more people?

Laws were broken and the criminals are still free

Americans did not have to kill thousands of Iraqis to get oil. They could buy oil there, just as other nations were doing. Who gives a government the green light to kill others to get an edge on others who are behaving properly? This happened in America when the decision was made to invade Iraq. Lies about finding weapons of mass destruction hid the motivation to steal oil from a little nation. And the perpetrators of these lies have not been brought to justice. Their acts resulted in the deaths of over one hundred thousand innocent Iraqis and the deaths of thousands of young soldiers from America and other nations. George W Bush and Dick Cheney should be tried in court as war criminals. Let justice come back to America.

American foreign policies have gone berserk

On September 12, 2011 Congressman Ron Paul made an outstanding condemnation of US foreign policy at the Republican presidential debate. He stated, "There's a difference between military spending and defense spending.

I'm tired of all the militarism we're involved in …I agree, we're in a lot of danger but most of the danger comes from a lack of wisdom in our foreign policy…We're under grave threat because we're occupying so many countries…What would we do if another country … say China … did to us what we do to all these countries over there?

Since we now can see that the US government has not learned its lesson and is still at war in Iraq, Afghanistan, Libya, Pakistan, Yemen, and who knows where else. Citizens of all nations must stand up and demand," Stop the slaughtering of our fellow citizens!" We all must stand up for all people who are being victimized by others. Warfare must be abolished. The world needs more nations to choose neutrality. No nation should have the right to build military bases on another nation's soil. No nation should have the right to dominate another nation. The world should arise and scream, "Enough is enough." " Get the Hell out of here!"

Believe it or not, the USA has over 900 military bases around the world! There are 227 bases in Germany, alone. These bases are not giving the USA more security. In fact, just the opposite is occurring. There is growing resentment over foreign troops being stationed in these countries. More and more of these nations are calling for these bases to be closed. The maintenance of these 900 bases is costing the USA $ 102 billion per year and rising.

The USA has over 100,000 troops in Afghanistan, and nobody can give a clear reason why. Originally, it was to catch Bin Laden. Well, he is now dead, and has not lived in Afghanistan for years! If the war is to stop terrorism, the reasoning is nuts. You cannot invade a country and continue to kill their citizens for over 10 years and expect the citizens to like you. The facts are that the USA is creating terrorists in Afghanistan. Declaring neutrality could be the greatest step to stop terrorist attacks on any nation.

The USA is becoming a greater target for terrorists by their efforts to dominate the world with over 900 military bases around the world. Dumb thinking. Do not do what we are doing is very good advice. US Admiral Mike Mullen, Chairman of the Joint Chiefs of Staff, stated ," the biggest threat to our national security is our debt." Perhaps, he should suggest that the USA stop trying to be the world's policeman. That would reduce the US debt by trillions of dollars.

The USA is now involved in 7 wars! They are in Iraq, Afghanistan, Pakistan, Libya, Yemen, Columbia, and Mexico. The very costly " war on drugs" in Columbia was started in 1971 by US President Richard Nixon. Hundreds of millions of dollars have been wasted on this so called war. This war includes the dropping from air planes of dangerous chemicals to kill the growth of drug bearing plants. Unfortunately, the fumes from these lethal chemicals are killing legal crops and endangering the lives of people that inhale these fumes. Columbia is still a dangerous country to visit because of the existence of drug cartels and their violence. The "war on drugs" has not been won.

In Mexico, the war on drugs is a calamity. Since December 2006 more than 35,000 people have been killed! The US government is providing arms and training to the Mexican military to fight the drug cartels. Since the US government repealed the ban on selling assault weapons, there has been a massive growth of gun violence in Mexico. In fact, the US is responsible for a flourishing sale of arms to members of the drug cartels. From 2009-2010, a report by a committee in the US Senate found that 70% of the guns seized in Mexico came from the USA. Of the 30,000 guns seized, 20,000 came from the USA. The USA sells more arms worldwide than any other nation. Some people are making a Hell of a lot of money by selling these guns. And I believe that the use of " Hell" belongs in this passage, as this lucrative business has caused a Hell for the victims of this increasing violence. The solution to this situation is obvious. There should be a worldwide ban on arms sales. No nation should be selling AK-47s and other dangerous arms to anybody. Selling arms results in lots of people being shot, maimed, and killed.

The "war on drugs" has morphed into the jailing of thousands of drug users

Some politicians have called for a legalization of drugs. I believe this is a formula for failure. The legalization of drugs would be a catastrophe for children, especially. But, it also would be very dangerous for people with mental health problems. And this population is growing, as the world problems are adding stress to millions of people struggling for survival.

I do not believe that people who use illegal drugs should be incarcerated. They need public programs to help them learn how to be happy naturally, and not by poisoning their bodies and brains for temporary highs.

I do believe that sellers of illegal drugs belong in jails. They are a threat to our children and to ourselves.

The nation of Sweden has a better idea. Their drug control policies combine balanced public health programs, and opposition to drug legalization. Cocaine use in Sweden is one fifth the use in the UK and Spain. We all need to study the Swedish programs and utilize them in our countries. Sweden's well funded public health programs are made possible by their not wasting tax dollars on military spending. Sweden is the oldest neutral nation in the world. They have been neutral since 1814.

We all have much to learn from Sweden

The economics alone is a very strong argument to declare Neutrality. Americans would save trillions of dollars by declaring Neutrality. I believe a Congressman or Senator should write," The US Neutrality Act" and present it for voting. I believe that a lot of thinking Americans would vote for neutrality. When you think about the location of America, what is there to defend against? On the north is Canada. Not much to be afraid of there. On the south is Mexico. They already have invaded the US and have at least 12 million Mexicans happily working and living in the USA. So I don't think America has much to fear there. So why is America spending so much needed funds on defense?

Are Americans better skilled than soldiers of other nations to spread democracy?

First part of the answer to this question is that the majority of American soldiers come from poverty stricken areas of the USA, and join the military because they do not qualify for other employment. Many of these American soldiers have never visited another country and lack any experience to deal with people different from themselves. Very few American soldiers can speak a foreign language. Few American soldiers have advanced educational backgrounds. Many American soldiers come from dysfunctional homes, and have experienced less kindness and caring than those of us fortunate enough to have been born with caring parents.

All of these handicaps combine to make American soldiers less able to recognize the good guys from the bad guys. American soldiers kill first when they are confused about the appearance and behaviour of foreign strangers.

The United Nations should be the real peace keeper, with the power to stop wars

American soldiers should not be the policemen of the world. In fact, no one nation should be shouldering the responsibilities of policing the entire world. This is a formula for failure. Policing of the world should be the responsibility of the United Nations. The UN should organize the world into regional police forces who are familiar with the citizens and governments of their region. These regional forces must have the resources and arms to stop any wrong doing in their part of the world. It is time to end NATO and surrender the policing to a world organization that is not dominated by any one nation.

The rules of the UN should be changed

No nation should be able to veto a law or action. Democracy should be the rule of law, not dictatorship by the USA or any other nation. Important decisions should be decided by a 2/3 vote. Other categories by 51%. The USA has only 5% of the world's population. It should not be fighting wars for the other 95%, or having military bases on any nation's soil, or dictating to the world. When international disputes erupt, both adversaries should take their dispute to an international court. Declarations of war should become buried in the dirt with so many other failed ways to treat each other cruelly.

The US Neutrality Act can be a huge engine for economic growth.

It would disarm the entire military, and put the generals and admirals to work on peaceful pursuits and end the planning for warfare. The dismissed soldiers should be given free education at high schools and universities so they can qualify for peaceful employment. The nuclear weapons should all be destroyed. That alone would save over $ 50 billion annually in maintenance of these terrible weapons. And this saving would be dwarfed by the other hundreds of billions of dollars freed to be spent for the many needs and protections of mankind.

As long as we continue to possess nuclear weapons, we motivate other nations to arm themselves too , in order to nullify our domination over them. How can we ask any nation to stop manufacturing nuclear weapons when we not only have the world's largest stockpile of these bad toys, but we are spending billions of dollars to maintain and modernize the delivery and killing capacities of our nuclear arms.

All military bases in America and all over the world should be closed. That would save hundreds of billions of dollars! All weapons should be destroyed. All agencies that are part of the military complex should be closed. This includes the CIA and the NSA. Anything that is related to militarism should become history. The CIA are notorious for assassinations and creating havoc amidst foreign elections. The NSA has an army of snoopers sticking their noses into communications around the world. All of this equals paranoia going berserk!

The trillions of dollars saved could be directed to defending the planet from Climate Change. This is a real threat to all nations of the world. The US government needs to hire lots of scientists to build a national grid for safe solar power. The US government should provide funding to invent solar machines that can provide electricity to each home and heat these homes as well. American businesses need to build a huge industry to supply safe energy, electric cars, and many new inventions for the world.

There should be a race to neutrality

Every nation should abandon nuclear energy and use of oil, gas, and coal. All nations must abandon their means to warfare. As there once was a race to the moon, there now should be a race to neutrality. If all nations pound their swords into plows, peace and prosperity can be shared by all. No nation should consider war as a solution to a problem. The UN must be the place to go to settle differences. As citizens go to the courts to settle differences, so should nations go to international courts to settle their differences. No nation should be allowed to dominate another nation. No government should be allowed to kill, maim, or torture their own citizens, or citizens from other nations. Capital punishment should be abolished in all countries. Enough is enough.

Militarism of a nation has a way of contaminating the culture of a nation.

The USA and some other nations have many sports based on violence. Boxing is one. Professional wrestling is another. Screened in fighting that allows kicking and pounding on a person while they are lying on the floor is another form of extremely violent sport that is televised daily into homes around the world. Beating a person on the ground has become an accepted behaviour by thugs. They now think nothing of repeatedly kicking their victims in the head while they lay on the ground. We can thank the lust for gold by TV stations for allowing this sadistic entertainment to be viewed by tens of millions of children. Gang beating of individuals resulting in fatalities and permanent brain damage are now the rage. This must stop. We must demand that it stop.

We must make the media stop training our children to be thugs. Sportsmanship should be substituted for outrageous viciousness. We have our work cut out for us. A village makes a child. We must protect good people from becoming bad people. We must not close our eyes to wrong doing. We must get together and work for peace not just among nations, but among people in schools, on the streets, and in homes. Violence must be confronted and defeated.

Do all Americans want war?

NO! Millions of us demonstrated against the war on Iraq. I was a speaker at a demonstration in Denver Colorado before a crowd of 30,000 people. I asked the crowd where they came from. The answers shouted were from cities all over the Rocky Mountain state. But, did the Senators of Colorado vote to stop the funding for the war. No, they voted to take more of our tax dollars and fund it. Was President Bush persuaded by the numerous huge demonstrations all over the USA to stop the march to war on Iraq? You know the answer to that one. He totally ignored the public clamor for peace. Maybe all of his appointments to the Administration, of oil and gas company executives, had a little bit to do with his decision.

Are Americans still opposed to the many wars the USA is involved in? YES. Many polls have shown that a vast majority of Americans oppose our participation in wars. In June 2011 the US Conference of Mayors of US cities voted and passed a resolution that supports efforts to speed up the ending of wars, requests the President and Congress to "bring these war dollars home to meet vital human needs."

When your government ignores public opinion, you've lost democracy!

And the US government no longer listens to the US public. Americans are no longer represented by their elected officials. We have lost our democracy. I will write more on this in a later chapter.

Meanwhile the CIA is doing more and more of their dirty work in Yemen and Pakistan, even though retiring Secretary of Defense, Robert Gates, stated in June 2011, "Enough is enough. These are wars of choice. Let's make a different choice."

The author, Greg Palast, entitled his book about America, " Armed Madhouse"

But, once the war machine is moving, it is tough to stop its momentum by a government saturated with bribery. Many Senators and Congressmen have a hard time saying no to all those big contributors from the US defense industry. It is not ignorance that drives the war machine. It is avarice, an insatiable desire for wealth and gain.

The US Neutrality Act would free lots of money to rebuild the failing infrastructure of the nation. This same act could provide scholarships to poor but bright students to go to college. This Act could rehire all of the teachers, police, firemen, and nurses who have been fired recently. This Act could provide e books and e readers and computers to every student so American education could once more be a model for other nations. And I believe the Neutrality Act could free billions of dollars which could be used to help people in poor nations become prosperous.

Will Neutrality endanger America?

The US government could use its new found wealth to help others instead of killing others. The whole image of America could change from being the dominator to being the common denominator for world peace. This change of image would eliminate any chance of a terrorist attack on America. Remember, that spending billions of dollars on defense did not stop 19 hijackers from bombing New York with our own air planes.

Defense spending will never protect your nation or the USA from terrorism. But changing nations' foreign policies can definitely provide security against terrorism. We must demand that our governments make changes in their foreign policies. The logic here is that if your government treats others with respect and caring, there are no grounds for desperate acts of terrorism. It is that simple.

The Middle East must be cooled down soon!

The world's most dangerous area for wars is the Middle East. And, not by coincidence, this is where the major oil reserves are located. If we are to achieve world peace, we must all change our government's policies in this area. And it better be done soon. Every nation in the world will be impacted if this area gets so hot that nuclear wars can break out and destroy our entire planet. So, pay attention. This involves you and you and you.

It is necessary to learn a little history lesson about this region to understand why this area is so important for us all to achieve world peace. After World War II, the world wanted to help the remaining Jews in the world, who had escaped the gas chambers of Nazi extermination camps.

The Holocaust is derived from the Greek word "holokauston", which means "sacrifice by fire." The persecution of Jews began in earnest in 1933 when Adolf Hitler was elected by the German voters. It ended in 1945 at the end of WW II. There were 6 concentration and extermination camps. The names of these camps were Chelmno, Belzec, Sobibo, Treblinka, Auschwitz, and Majdanek. 11 million men, women, and children were killed in these camps. The Germans targeted Jews, Gypsies, Gays, Jehovah's Witnesses, disabled, and dissenters. Two thirds of the Jews in Europe were murdered in these camps. The total of Jews killed was over 6 million! 1.1 million children were murdered in these camps.

The partitioning of Palestine started the problems that are still not settled, 64 years later!

On November 29, 1947 the UN General Assembly voted 33-13, with 10 abstentions, to partition Palestine into two entities, an Israeli state and an Arab state. The surrounding Arab nations did not support this partition. Wars broke out several times, and ultimately the Israelis won their independence. Today, 20% of the population of Israel is still composed of Palestinians. They have voting rights, but are deprived of other civil rights. Millions of Palestinians have been displaced by the partitioning and the many wars between the Israelis and the surrounding Arab nations.

Lots of nuclear bombs lying around here

Over the years, the USA has given many billions of dollars in aid to the nation of Israel. Today the US military and the Israeli military share military intelligence and have bonded together on several aspects of military functions. Israel has a large presence of nuclear arms. These are not the only places that nuclear arms exist in this area. Close by are 2 nations with nuclear weapons, Pakistan and India. And between Iraq and Pakistan lies Iran, who may also be close to becoming another nation with nuclear arms.

India is not a signatory to the Nuclear Non-Proliferation Treaty. In fact, they are building a fleet of nuclear armed submarines. Larsen and Toubro, India's largest defense contractor, is contracted to develop a launcher for a nuclear-tipped submarine-launched cruise missile.

Pakistan is a very unstable nation, that possesses nuclear weapons. The CIA's drone warfare in Pakistan is killing both militants and lots of Pakistani civilians. The Pakistanis do not love America. They hate us. They are a breeding ground for terrorists. We killed Bin Laden in Pakistan. We should get the Hell out of there, quick. We are there now, at our own peril.
India and Pakistan do not like each other. They have almost gone to war several times over the territory of Kashmir. Both nations want Kashmir. Terrorists from Pakistan have set off bombs in India, and have been responsible for the deaths of numerous Indian civilians.

So, when I say this is a dangerous area and capable of starting WWIII, I am by no means exaggerating.

Israel's only ally is the USA, and this relationship is troubling.

On June 5, 2011, Meir Dagan, Mossad chief, disclosed some alarming information about the leadership of Israel. (Mossad is the Israeli Institute for Intelligence and Special Operations. It is similar to the CIA). Mr. Dagan recently retired, along, with the head of Shin Bet security service, the head of military intelligence, and the chief of staff of the armed forces. He stated that the loss of these 4 retired Israeli leaders would remove any barrier to the " reckless and irresponsible" leaders, Prime Minister Benjamin Netanyahu and Defense Minister Ehud Barak. Mr. Dagan warned the public that the remaining two leaders might attack Iran, which could be a threat to the survival of the nation of Israel. He also warned that the absence of any type peace initiative by Israel could isolate the nation and cause reckless action by Netanyahu and Ehud Barak against Iran.

Israeli attacking Iran makes no sense. The president of Iran, Mahmoud Ahmadinejad, is on the way out of power. Recently, he has been publicly humiliated by the real power brokers of Iran, the Islamist clerics. These clerics intentionally made the presidency weak when it was created. The supreme leader of Iran is Ayatollah Ali Khamenei. He picked Ahmadinejad to be president and is now opposing his efforts to remain as president.

The serious meddling in Iranian politics by the US caused much suffering.

Iranians' animosity toward the USA dates back to August 19, 1953 when the UK and the US CIA staged a coup that displaced their first democratically elected Prime Minister, after hundreds of years of harsh tyrannies by monarchies. Dr. Mossadegh was elected in 1951. He was beloved by the Iranian people. Prime Minister Mossadegh created unemployment compensation. He required factory owners to pay benefits for injured and sick workers. He put a stop to forced labor on landlords' estates.

Mossadegh also nationalized the Anglo-Iranian Oil Company. The Iranian nation had been robbed of much of their natural resources by the English and the Russians. The US took part in the coup after President Eisenhower was manipulated into thinking that Mossadegh was leading Iran into communism, which would have been impossible against the strength of the Islamic clerics. (One of the actions of communist governments was to forbid the practices of religion.) Obviously Eisenhower had no real knowledge of the strength of the Clerics in Iran.

The US government has a history of meddling in other nations' governments.

This intrusion into the government of a foreign nation is despicable behaviour. Was it the first and only time that the US government has perpetrated such a crime? Unfortunately it was one of many times. William Blum, an investigative journalist, wrote a book entitled, " Rogue State." On page 1 of his book, I quote his words, " Between 1945 and 2005 the United States has attempted to overthrow more than 50 foreign governments, and attempted to crush more than 30 populist-nationalist movements struggling against intolerable regimes. In the process, the US has caused the end of life for several million people, and condemned many millions more to a life of agony and despair."

This unsavory behaviour was never reported in the history books I was required to read as a young student. I am sure that most Americans are as uninformed as I was of this past history of our country. I believe that this conduct by the US government came back to bite it when the terrorists bombed New York and the Pentagon building in the nation's capitol.

How corporations have invaded the US government and caused havoc around the world.

In June 2011, 2,000 classified US diplomatic cables were released by Wiki Leaks to the US and international media pertaining to the US meddling big time in the nation of Haiti. These leaks disclosed how 3 large US clothing manufacturers, Fruit of the Loom, Hanes, and Levi's, worked with the US government to block an increase in the minimum wage in Haiti. Haiti is one of the very poorest nations in the world! Let's look at that again. Three rich corporations and the richest nation in the world conspire to keep the people in very poor Haiti from having an increase in their minimum wage!

 Did this behaviour help American workers? NO- because they had already lost their jobs to the poor workers in Haiti. So, this was certainly not an action based on national interests. It was most certainly based on the interests of three corporations and their lust for profits- at the cost of the lives of the poorest of the poor in the world.

And why did the US government help these greedy corporations? Could bribery be the cause? Why else would government officials try to suppress the minimum wage of poor people in a far away land? Is this kind of behaviour going to protect American citizens from terrorist attacks, or is this going to contribute toward terrorist attacks? The answer is simple. Corruption in US foreign policy threatens the security of US citizens.

In 2004 the US government was deeply involved in creating a coup that removed the democratically elected President of Haiti, Jean-Bertrand Aristide. The US government was responsible for the kidnapping of President Aristide and preventing his return to Haiti. The US government also recently supported an election in Haiti that deliberately banned the participation in the election of Haiti's largest opposition party, Lavalas, which is the party of Jean-Bertrand Aristide! These actions are by the US government who constantly harps to the world that their wars are meant to produce democracy around the world.

Most governments, including the US government, need a spanking for their bad behaviour.

American politicians are mostly cowards who do not like to lead, and are mostly interested in getting reelected. Let's hope you readers establish much better standards for electing quality leadership. I now believe that the US President and the US Congress should issue a strong apology to the people of Iran for our destruction of their democracy under the leadership of Dr. Mossadegh. I can assure you that the students of Iran are very familiar with the meddling in their government by the USA and UK. No nation should try to dominate another nation. I am sure that the presence of oil in Iran was the motivation for the English to encourage US President Eisenhower to do their dirty work for them.

Besides a public apology, the US government needs to totally revise their foreign diplomacy. It is essential that this is done soon. The US has made a lot of enemies around the world.

The distancing of the US government from militarism would be a concrete step in the right direction.

We citizens of the world must recognize that we are now entering a time that has never before been experienced. The blunt warnings by Mother Nature with her severe storms and droughts are stark warnings of Climate Change.

The proliferation of planet ending nuclear weapons is evidence that we all have much to do to protect our children from annihilation.
The decisions to go to war must be banned from the greasy hands of bribed politicians. We, all citizens of the world, must march against nationalism. We must stop considering people a few feet across a border line as " them", and

not as " us." Wars between nations must be considered out of date. We must open the minds of millions, so their thinking is not burdened with self destructive and archaic leanings toward violence. Violence must not be the last resort. It must never be a resort. Intellectual advancement over old beliefs must prevail. You do not have to go to a college to think 'out of the box'. We no longer should tolerate repeating cerebral blunders of the past.

I honestly believe that we can right this ship of citizens of the world- if we open our minds and then proceed to open the minds of others. Thinking can be fun. It can be enlightening. It may just save our planet for our children and our grand children. We all have a job to do-now.

Americans must recognize that our military presence is raising the threat of terrorism towards us, and even worse!

Looking on a map, one can see that Iran is bordered by Iraq, Afghanistan, and Pakistan. All three of these border nations have no love for Israel's big ally, the USA. The US has armies in Iraq and Afghanistan, and is guilty of sending drones to bomb areas in Pakistan on a frequent basis. More and more civilians have been killed by these drone bombers in Pakistan. A poll taken of Pakistan citizens found that they were <u>more</u> sympathetic to Al Qaeda than to the USA!

The Pakistan military is very resistant to fighting against the Taliban because they believe that they are fighting America's war against their own people. The drone attacks in Pakistan are operated by the CIA. The Pakistanis have blocked the shipments of food and water to the base used for drone attacks! It is probably only a matter of time before the drone war is stopped completely by the Pakistan military. General Kayani of Pakistan has already informed the director of the CIA that Pakistan would not allow independent operations by the CIA. The poor relations between Pakistan and the USA is a real threat to the US and Israeli security. Pakistan has nuclear weapons!

If Israel were to attack Iran, there could be a regional war that could involve nuclear bombs coming from Israel, Pakistan, India, and possibly Iran. And, of course from the USA! Israel could easily be responsible for pulling the USA into any war that they start. This is the risk that George Washington warned Americans about in his farewell address. This could happen if we do not put real restraints on Israel – now!

This is a formula for the destruction of our planet.

Remember, one volcano eruption can stop air traffic in large areas of the world. What do you think will happen if nuclear bombs start exploding in this very explosive environment? We, all of us, cannot sit by and do nothing with this dire warning from the very important retired chief of Mossad in Israel.

I propose that the citizens of Israel throw out leaders who only think of war as a solution to problems. I also propose that not only Israeli citizens, but citizens from all nations make sure that their laws keep the military under the control of civilian leaders, and not the reverse. All nations must strive to have Separation of Military and State. Generals should not be making decisions to go to war. Citizens must have this power. It is much too easy to start a war today. Let's make it so hard that there are no more wars.

Israel's reckless history begs for more restraint by big brother America

Israel has displayed reckless and ruthless behaviour in the past. In 1982 Ariel Sharon was Defense Minister of Israel. One night in 1982, Sharon and the Israeli army surrounded two Palestinian refugee camps in Lebanon. The Israeli army shot up flares every 60 seconds during the night while their allies, entered two refugee camps, called Sabra and Shatila, and raped and stabbed women, and slaughtered between 2,000 and 3,000 unarmed women, children, and elderly male refugees! This occurred over 3 days, Sept. 16-18, 1982. The bodies were buried in mass graves. Israeli officers watched the slaughter from the roof tops of surrounding buildings.

Ariel Sharon was removed from office after an Israeli court found him guilty of war crimes. However, the people of Israel elected this monster in 2001 to be their Prime Minister! In January, 2006 Sharon suffered a stroke and retired as PM on April 14, 2006. He has been in a coma since Jan. 2006. Even though this debacle occurred in 1982, most Arabs are still quite familiar with what happened in the refugee camps, Sabra and Shatila,

Gaza. Shame on the world for its silence

Palestinians living in Gaza between December 17, 2008 and January 18, 2009 are certainly reminded of this because once more civilians are being murdered in very large numbers by Israeli forces. During this short period of time, Israeli tanks, drones, attack helicopters, and attack air planes killed 1,400 people in Gaza! 85% were civilians! 535 were women and children. Over 10 mosques were bombed. Schools and universities were bombed. A dozen hospitals were bombed. A vegetable open market crowded with shoppers was bombed! Many ambulances were bombed and shot up by the Israeli army.

And for those of you unfamiliar with drones, they contain very powerful visual instruments that operators in far away safe buildings can see their targets quite precisely. They can tell the difference between a man and woman and a child. They can see the aftermath of their targeted killings, too. The technology of drones has been created in advanced laboratories in Israel. These murders were committed behind walls of secrecy.

The USA is spending our tax dollars on more instruments of destruction

The manufacturing of drones is not isolated to Israel. The American government is heavily into research for developing drones of all sizes and shapes. They are spending billions of US tax dollars in developing smaller and smaller drones that can spy on people and kill people. They are developing drones that can be manufactured to look like bugs and birds. So the next time you feed a humming bird, make sure you are fully clothed.

Oh, I wish this were fiction, but it sadly exposes how far down the chute America is sliding. And how dangerous their research poses for the world. The drones are capable of spying on an entire city! This will require over 2,000 analysts to process this data. The paranoia driving this madness must be addressed. US tax payers should become a lot more curious of how their tax dollars are being diverted from killing bugs who spread diseases to metallic bugs who can carry poison to deliberately kill people.

The virtual imprisoning of the people of Gaza behind concrete walls and the blockading their assess to food, medical supplies, and exports is another example of an unrestrained ally, Israel, gone berserk.

The Israeli government has occupied and blockaded 1.5 million Palestinian people inside Gaza since 2006. Since the Palestinians elected the Hamas party to represent them, the Israelis have used all sorts of cruelty to punish these people for voting for a different political party! Yes, you read that right. One nation is punishing another nation for democratically electing a different political party!

And the rest of the western world has sat on their fingers and done nothing to stop these crimes against humanity. This blockade has prevented the foreign Press from witnessing the slaughtering of innocents within the walls of the blockade. The blockade consists of concrete walls with watch towers staffed with armed guards, just like a prison. There also is barbed wire and the proximate fields are filled with land mines!

On September 19, 2007, the Israeli Security Cabinet declared Gaza a " hostile entity." This declaration enabled Israel to restrict the flow of supplies of fuel and electricity. By labeling a state of 1.5 million people a hostile entity, they were condemning an entire group of people, rather than focusing on the minority of actual militants who were guilty of firing rockets into Israel.

This mass condemnation has severely damaged the economy of Gaza. The blockade also stopped 100% of all exports. 90% of the businesses have closed. There is a severe shortage of food. Even bread and water are scarce. The population of Gaza has 750,000 children. Most of the children are gravely suffering from malnutrition. The citizens depend on donations to survive. Medicines and parts to medical devices are vitally needed to save lives.

The Israeli army has destroyed many ambulances carrying sick and wounded to the hospitals. The Israeli army has attacked UN aid convoys carrying food and medicines. They have attacked schools filled with students. Thousands of houses have been bombed with people crammed inside.

After ordering an Israeli tank to fire its guns into several floors of one building with people inside, the tank finally stopped shooting. A mother and grandmother waving a white flag, accompanied by three children aged 2, 4, and 7 walked out of the front door. A soldier shot the grandmother twice, and shot all 3 children. Two of the children were killed.

The 4 year, old named Samar, was shot in the back and is now permanently paralyzed below the waist. A BBC journalist , Christian Fraser, investigated the story of Samar and confirmed the above facts. He also learned that one child had 10 bullets in her chest. He also discovered that a man with a horse pulling a cart tried to save the stricken grandmother. He was shot dead, as was his horse. When an ambulance arrived on the scene, it was destroyed also. There were no Palestinian militants or guns or ammunition found in the blood soaked house.

These were acts of ethnic cleansing, a very serious war crime.

The small nation of Norway, at first like most other western nations, believed that Israel was the victim and that all Palestinians were terrorists. Slowly, the Norwegians began to learn differently. Their sources were from Norwegian doctors who had been volunteering for several years to enter Gaza and work in hospitals there treating the victims of actions by the Israeli army.

Two brave doctors from Norway, Erik Fosse and Mads Gilbert, wrote a book entitled, " Eyes in Gaza." I found this book in a small library in New Zealand. During their time in Gaza, they were interviewed by various members of the international media by phone calls and by email. The Israeli government learned of these interviews and tried to stop the interviews. When these two doctors were leaving Gaza they were stranded at a border station for 24 hours. For the first time this station was violently bombed by Israeli war planes. Fortunately, the two doctors were not harmed and escaped from Gaza to tell the world of what they had been witnessing. After each bombing, these doctors had been treating almost exclusively civilians! The great majority of the victims of these bombing raids were innocents, and the majority were children.

The lack of restraint by the US government over Israeli transgressions has exposed the USA to wide spread animosity around the world.

And Israel, flush with American dollars and American military arms and know how has again and again displayed total disdain for the destruction and the suffering that their war machine has wreaked on innocent people around the Middle East. After the cease fire in the 2006 war against Lebanon, Israeli attack planes dropped over one million cluster bombs on Lebanese residential areas. And I said, "after the cease fire!" Many of these bombs do not explode on impact, and are left for children to pick up and be maimed or killed as they explode. Most of the world has condemned the use of cluster bombs and land mines, but the US government has ignored their actions and continues to manufacture these horrendous weapons against humanity. And, of course, they continue to ship these weapons to Israel.

Israel would not exist if the US government did not support them. And I am not suggesting that the US government cease supporting Israel. What I am suggesting is that the US government draws a line between defense and unrestrained cruelty. Between defense and genocide. Between defense and murdering innocent people. And the US government could easily restrain Israel.

We could make demands to stop the blockade of Gaza. We could say, tear down the illegal settlements on Palestinian lands. We could say tear down the wall over Palestinian lands. We could stop manufacturing land mines and cluster bombs and distributing them to Israel. And if Israel refused to listen, we could threaten them with withholding any future funding for military supplies or other forms of aid.

We could also make it clear that if they attack Iran, they are on their own, as we forbid their trying to get the US into a war that they deliberately started. And if the US government does not get tough with Israel, we can expect ourselves soon to be fighting in Iran and eventually cleaning up some American cities after some parties in the world decide to deliver nuclear bombs across the border and explode them in US cities.

The best advice for American foreign policy came way back in time from the first President, George Washington, in his farewell speech on September 19, 1796. "Observe good faith and justice towards all nations. Cultivate peace and harmony with all. In the execution of such a plan nothing is more essential than that permanent, inveterate antipathies against particular nations and passionate attachments for others, should be excluded; and that, in place of them, just and amicable feelings towards all should be cultivated. The nation , which indulges towards another an habitual hatred or an habitual fondness, is in some degree a slave."

Is Howard Greenebaum anti-Semitic? Was Moses?

By now some of you readers may be curious about me the author of the book you are reading. You may be asking yourself, " Is Greenebaum anti-Semitic?". So let's clear that up quickly. I was born of Jewish parents. I was bar mitzvahed at the age of 13 at Har Sinai Temple where my father served as Vice President of the Congregation. I have spent many years of my life as an advocate for civil rights for all peoples. I do not favor any one race. I only favor the Human Race. I have won the Democratic Party's nomination to the US Congress twice, both times losing to heavily funded Republican incumbents.

In 1982, which was my first try for public office, I was busy selling tickets to a large fundraiser for my campaign. I had received endorsements from many Maryland politicians who had said that they would attend my fundraiser. When I learned of the slaughters of thousands of innocent Palestinians in the refugee camps, Sabra and Shatila, I was very angry. I decided that I had established a liaison with the Press and I should use this opportunity to voice my condemnation of this ruthless conduct by the Israeli army. Shortly after I had voiced my opinion, almost every politician who had endorsed me, cancelled their acceptance to my fundraiser. I felt that I had destroyed any opportunity that I would ever have of contributing to the good of my nation in Congress.

Then a week later I received a letter from US Congressman Parren Mitchell. He invited me to visit him in his office at the capitol in Washington. When I walked into his busy office he came out of his private office and told his aides to hold all calls. I sat with Congressman Mitchell for over one hour. Nobody disturbed us. He complimented me on my stand for the oppressed and encouraged me to continue to run for office. This kindness by a very busy US Congressman has steadied my drive to devote my talents and energy towards helping not only my country but yours as well. Parren Mitchell was one of the few Congressmen who never wasted any time on fundraising. He spent all of his time trying to help people. His total spending for campaigns averaged $5,000. That may be a record. I do not know.

Congressman Mitchell's family was quite active in the civil rights organization, the NAACP. The actual title is the National Association for the Advancement of Colored People. Congressman Mitchell was of African American heritage. The NAACP now has a very large membership, but few people are familiar with the original founders. The first president was white. Several of the founders were white. Although the NAACP was founded in 1909, the first president to be African American was not elected until 1975. Many Jewish Americans have been members of the NAACP, including myself. Jewish Americans and African Americans have bonded over their mutual fights against bigotry.

When I was campaigning for Congress, I was a frequent guest at African American churches. I was always invited by the Minister to come up on the podium and speak to the congregation. It was an honor that I will never forget. I owe much to people like Parren Mitchell who helped me continue to fight for the good of people. In 1982 ,after the election, I received a letter from the Maryland Attorney General, Stephen H. Sachs, stating, " I know that it hurts to lose, but I wanted to tell you that you have my respect and gratitude for all that you have done for the political process." Two years after I had lost in the 1982 Primary Election, I won my first Democratic nomination to the US Congress in 1984. After I lost in the General Election, I received a letter from US Senator Edward M. Kennedy stating, " Just a note to commend you for the effective race that you ran against difficult odds. I look forward to working with you in the future, and know that you will continue to serve the public interest." Before the 1988 General Election I received a letter from the California Attorney General, John Van De Kamp, stating," I am happy to add my name to the long list of people endorsing you for Congress."

After the 1988 elections it was discovered that only 6 of the 435 seats in the US House of Representatives had changed hands! And of the six incumbents who lost , four were being charged for crimes, and one may have gone to jail. I believe one of the other two died. With this serious lack of turnover, both the Republican and Democratic challengers assembled in a historic meeting in St. Louis, Missouri. The national press gave the meeting a lot of attention.

After I had an opportunity to speak at this meeting, several of the challengers encouraged me to write a book about this historic non-election. I wrote the book, "Free Elections ???" and self published it in 1990. The cover of the book depicted an American flag with a hole in it. $100 bills were flowing through the hole in the flag. I hired a high school student, Tommy Merriman, to help me drive and we drove 13,000 miles in 68 days. I lectured at universities and appeared at book signings around the USA. I also appeared as a guest on 210 radio talk shows discussing my book for an hour each time. The total sales of my book was 9,000. It is too bad more people did not read it, as it had several solutions that could have prevented some of the problems facing us today. And unfortunately, American politics has become even more corrupt than 21 years ago.

I hope that all of you readers are now convinced that I am about as far from being anti-Semitic as Moses was. When former US President Jimmy Carter condemned the treatment of the Palestinians by the Israelis, he was called anti-Semitic. This name calling can be very effective to sway the public when a national media does not inform the public of the facts. It is all of our responsibility to never accept the lies of propagandists. We must always maintain a defense against liars who are paid to defame people who are working for the good of us all. I might add that I do not believe that any group of any race or religious group should shield criminals from the law. I believe that is not in the best interest of the group, or in the best interest of protecting the public from further criminal acts by the perpetrator.

Israeli citizens have been deceived by leaders playing on their fears. They have allowed their corrupt leaders to steal land from defenseless Palestinians under the guise that this was for national security. They have allowed their corrupt leaders to manipulate them by planting fear into their minds. Every act of stealing land and cruelty is defended by calling these crimes necessary for national security. American readers of this book may find these lies familiar. How many times have we Americans been propagandized with the words, " for our national interest". Unfortunately, we never had those "national interests" identified. Below you will find no person better qualified to expose these interests than a tough old US marine general, named Smedley D. Butler. In 1935 the most decorated US soldier, Marine General Smedley D. Butler, wrote a book called, " War is a Racket." Here are a couple quotes of General Smedley Butler, " Why don't those damned oil companies fly their own flags on their personal property-maybe a flag with a gas pump on it." On the cover of his book he stated, " I spent 33 years in the Marines, most of the time being a high-class muscle man for big business, for Wall Street and the bankers. In short, I was a racketeer for Capitalism."

I believe every young man and woman considering becoming a soldier should first read General Butler's book. Nobody better understood the basis of wars than General Butler.

Gaza is still imprisoned

As I am writing this book, the conditions for the people in Gaza are worsening. Hospitals in Gaza are cancelling operations because the Israeli blockade has stopped the shipments of medical supplies. Gaza has now been under blockade for over 5 years! The UN is unable to do anything because the US continues to veto any real response to this cruelty.

The population behind this blockade is growing. These young people are witnessing the cruelty of the Israeli military. And they know of the support of the Israelis by the USA. 72 % of 15-19 year olds are unemployed! 66% of 20-24 year olds are unemployed! These children have witnessed the killings of their families and their friends. The Israeli blockade is building an army of very motivated soldiers in Gaza! The Israeli blockade is more of a threat to Israeli citizens than it will ever be a source of security. Violence begets violence. The USA is far more at risk from terrorist attacks now than before the blockade was erected. Blind support of Israel is definitely not in the best interests of the American people. Support for Israel must always include restraint of Israel. Israelis must learn to overcome their fears, and embrace their neighbors. Easy to say, but nevertheless, quite necessary to secure peace in a much troubled part of the world.

There are people like Jimmy Carter who could teach the Israelis how to live in peace with their neighbors. He is a man that both sides can trust.

There have been many attempts from around the world to stop the Israeli blockade of Gaza, and other Israeli transgressions

In November 2008 the UN High Commission for Human Rights called for an end of the Israeli blockade of Gaza. 5 weeks later, Israel began bombing Gaza.

Israel is violating the Fourth Geneva Convention of 1949's rules which forbid punishing innocent people for actions that they have not personally committed. Israel ratified this convention in 1949. Israeli settlements on the West Bank also violate the 4th Geneva convention.

Israel has broken 28 Security Council resolutions and broken about 100 resolutions of the General Assembly of the UN.

In 2004 the International Court of Justice in The Hague in a vote of 14-1 ruled that the wall erected across the West Bank violated international law and should be taken down.

The US government supported Israel against all of the above attempts to stop the lawless and ruthless behaviour of the Israeli government. The US government has acted like an appeasing parent who refuses to restrain her/his child from bad behaviour.

On April 22, 2009, six lawyers in Norway filed charges against the leaders of the government of Israel and the military leaders involved in the invasion of Gaza. The lawyers stated," There can be no doubt that all subjects knew about, had considered the consequences of, and ordered or approved the criminal acts. At the very least, they failed to stop the contraventions when they became aware of them, despite being able to do so." The Norwegian Bar Association's Human Rights Committee has supported the complaint.

And in June 2011 a flotilla of 10 boats of people from over 20 countries attempted to confront the blockade of Gaza. Some of the boats were sabotaged while in ports. The US State Department and the Israeli government persuaded the Greek government to stop the ships from going to Gaza.

Advice to Israel, " A little humility never hurt anyone."

In 2010 a smaller group tried to sail past the blockade and the Israelis killed 9 people and injured 50 others. Israel refused to apologize to Turkey, whose citizens had been killed in this attack. Israel's refusal to apologize has turned Turkey from an ally to an enemy. Not smart. Arrogance is not the answer.

The American government must wake up and stop writing blank checks to governments around the world. This is not working. The US government must stop Israel from shooting itself in the foot. Cruel treatment of the Palestinians is not only making them your enemies, but it is turning the whole world against Israel and their big brother, the US.

In a few days the UN will vote whether to declare Palestine a State and entitled to some of the services from the UN. The US government is trying to persuade nations to vote against the rights of Palestinians. I believe Israel has an opportunity to show its humanity in this situation. Israel should tell the US to stop electioneering, and declare its support for Palestine. Israel should also tear down the walls around Gaza and work toward inclusion of Palestinians. These reversals in foreign policy could serve as giant first steps towards lasting peace in the Mideast.

The UN must repeal the power to veto. The veto is a stumbling block to peace.

The relatives of the victims of the Holocaust have stumbled into creating a Holocaust for Palestinians in Gaza! What a mistake this is for Israel. No nation should be allowed to do what Israel is now doing to Gaza. We must all demand that this behaviour be stopped. No people of any race deserves to be annihilated by another. The rules of the UN must be changed. Vetoes by a single nation should be abolished. The UN needs to be a democracy of all nations. And the UN must be given the means to stop genocide by any nation.

Wars can be stopped if we all act smarter.

Tyrants are easily recognized. Stop them in their tracks. Don't believe their lies. Kick them out of power. The Israeli citizens should kick the warriors out of office, and elect people dedicated to peace.

Wars are started for only a few reasons. One certainly is for oil. Did you know that in 1999 there was a discovery of huge reserves of natural gas off the coast of Gaza? There is 1.3 trillion cubic feet of natural gas there! And there could be oil sitting down there also. So when the Israeli navy set up a naval blockade off Gaza's coast, what was their real purpose? Stopping supplies of food and medicines or babysitting the gas and oil?

We need international courts to protect every nation from other nations stealing their natural resources.

It happened in Iran. It happened in Africa. It has happened all over the world under the name of colonialism. Under the name of empire. It is wrong. It causes wars. People get killed. We all need to learn to pay for things we desire. Stealing is bad. By people. And yes by governments, too.

Citizens of every nation should consider the costs of their defense spending versus the costs necessary for other purposes, such as health care, education, expansion of infrastructure, and maintenance of infrastructure, etc. Isn't there a better way to defend a nation from war than going to war? We all are wasting a whole lot of money depending on armies to defend us. It would be much cheaper to hire lawyers!

Lets eliminate poverty instead of our fellow man.

Yes, we need a police force, but it would be much, much cheaper to give this responsibility to the UN. The UN should be given the complete responsibility to stop invasions of nations by other nations. The UN must be given the resources and manpower to keep the world in peace. So individual nations may declare neutrality and surrender all of their man killing instruments.

Just think of this scenario. All the nations in one continent declare neutrality, and destroy all of their weapons. No weapons. No wars. It is that simple. Imagine all the money that will then be available to raise the standard of living for all people living in this continent. And if one continent can raise their standard of living so high, why should not all continents follow this path to prosperity, and to peace?

" WE WILL NEVER GET A CLEAN ENVIRONMENT WITH A DIRTY GOVERNMENT".....H. GREENEBAUM

We all must connect the dots.

When I was younger and quite active in the environmental movement, I often heard environmentalists state that they did not want to get involved in politics. I tried to explain to them that depending on public demonstrations, alone, will never result in change. We must demand that our government protect our environment. And we must stop the bribery that is getting in the way of this protection. This certainly involves all of us paying a lot more attention to whom we vote for . We need representatives who are honest and we can depend on, to vote for the public interest. We must pass laws that stop the bribery in order to achieve protection for our planet. There will be more information on this in a later chapter in this book.

With only 5% of the world's population, America succeeds in polluting 25% of the world!

That's telling 'em big ole Superpower. And at every world conference, we proudly strut in and never sign up for anything. No caps on pollution. No caps on corporations' dirty droppings. And we are supposed to be a world leader. With leadership like this, Mother Nature is laughing her head off, while spitting out tornadoes, floods, droughts, hurricanes, tsunamis, earth quakes, landslides, and lava out of volcanoes! All increasing in severity, as per the Climate Change warnings issued by scientists around the world.

Since I am an American, I have learned far more about my country, in my 82 years, than I know about your country. And I admit that my country is responsible for 25% of the world's pollution. However, you guys are responsible for the other 75%! So don't go whistling Dixie, and think America can fix the whole mess. You readers must soak up this vital information and teach others.

Force your governments to be responsible for their corporations' pollution of everyone's air and water.

Winds blow the dirt from all of our factories to all of the world. The planet is rotating under this mess. When you dirty the ocean off your coast, we get to eat fish from your trash. In a few words, we all must shoulder the responsibility of protecting our planet.

Climate Change is here and we all are witnessing it happening all around the world. Scientists predicted storms would be more severe. Storms are now more severe. If you don't believe this statement, ask the people in Japan. Or the people in Pakistan where 20% of their country was under water from flooding. Or the people in Southeastern USA where hundreds of tornadoes tore apart cities and killed hundreds of people. Or the people in Queensland, Australia where history breaking flooding covered mass amounts of this area-equal to all of Germany and France, combined. Or China where over 24,000 villages have been abandoned because of desert expansion!

Cap and Trade is a Scam!

So, what are we doing about this threat to mankind? The world's largest polluter, the USA, introduced a scheme called, " Cap and Trade" during the 1990s during the first international conference on combating Climate Change. No other nation was interested in this scheme but they all bowed to the "wisdom" of the great polluter, the USA. Unfortunately, the USA did not sign on for any of the restraints to pollution, and left the conference with only this scheme on their hands. For 20 years Cap and Trade has been ballyhooed as the answer to reducing skyward pollution. The many nations that have jumped into this snake pit have thrown around a lot of money but it has not brought any relief from pollution of our atmosphere.

The guiding "principle" (and I use the word "principle" loosely) is that polluting corporations buy carbon credits from non-polluting corporations and this money is supposed to reward these non-polluters and in some way cause a reduction in pollution over our heads. Or they buy carbon credits from poor countries and supposedly help them cut their pollution. Very few of these projects have materialized.

The world is getting more polluted, as bribery flourishes, and Climate Change kills more people.

You will notice that the polluting corporations are not required to actually reduce their polluting! They simply buy these pieces of paper and go on polluting like they always have before. For 20 years this nutty scheme has been operating. And guess what, the amount of pollution rising skyward has increased by leaps and bounds! Big surprise, eh. And the biggest polluter, the USA, has never even tried this scheme, even though it was the entity that created it. As of June, 2011 the USA has not passed one bill to cut emissions. In fact, the Republicans who control the US House of Representatives are trying to cut funding for the US Environmental Protection Agency (EPA) and weaken environmental regulations. This is what happens when a political party gets saturated with bribes from polluting corporations, and from corporations who make huge profits selling fools' fuels (oil, gas, and coal).

The world trade in these phony pieces of paper has reached $ 144 billion through the EU Emissions Trading system. 95% of these trades were with the EU ETS in 2010. It is estimated that 20%to 90% (quite a range) of these trades have no effect on emission reduction. Over 100 people have been charged with fraud in these trades. And the scheme is now a victim of unregulated speculation around the world. These pieces of paper should be converted into toilet paper. At least then they would actually be utilized to rid the world of certain emissions.

It is time to stop playing with these pieces of paper and treating Climate Change like a game of "Monopoly". (Monopoly is a game for children with fake paper dollars that has been very popular for years in the USA.) It is time to put some Common Sense into this grave threat to mankind. Polluting the air and water is the same as poisoning the air and water. Nobody wants to breathe poisoned air or drink poisoned water. It can kill you. A person who deliberately poisons you is guilty of a crime. They get arrested and go to jail.

That is the simple answer to stop the poisoning of our air and water. We must treat this behaviour as a criminal offense and charge the perpetrators and have them arrested.

Any executive of any corporation who is responsible for poisoning our air or water should be arrested, tried in court, and if found guilty, be sent to prison.

There should be clear, precise laws written that prohibit the polluting or our air and water. These laws must clearly indicate what the crimes are and how the perpetrator has chosen to ignore the law. These laws should be publicized and all corporations should pay for government inspections to indicate the violations with a time period to correct these violations. The executives at these corporations should be given documents that describe the violations, with a list of contractors who can fix the problem. If the quotes for mitigation are higher than a certain percentage of the gross sales of the corporation, then the government then should offer some sort to subsidy to help the corporation pay for the required mitigation.

We must not trust executives of corporations to keep anti-pollution equipment operating.

A friend of mine used to sell this anti-pollution equipment to US corporations. Some corporations bought the equipment, but a funny thing happened when my friend happened to visit his clients without prior notice. The machines were not operating. The power was deliberately turned off. So, we must learn from my friend's experience.

Governments must inspect corporations and verify that these machines are keeping our air clean. These inspections should never be requested in advance. They must be done by surprise so they cannot turn on the machines for the inspections, and turn them off again when the inspector leaves. The inspections should be paid for by the corporations, not by our tax dollars. If a corporation is found deliberating turning off the equipment, the executives responsible should be charged with a major crime, arrested, and if found guilty in court, sentenced to jail time. It is a waste of time to just fine corporations. Executives laugh at fines and continue to do their dirty deeds. Nobody laughs at jail time.

There also should be a technological connection to the anti-pollution machines that connects to a regional governmental inspection station. If the anti-pollution machine is turned off, an alarm sounds at the inspection station. The violator is then called to ascertain if this is a maintenance turn off or a mechanical problem. With this set up, we should be able to keep the violations at a minimum.

If our governments push installations of safe energy, such as solar or wind, many corporations may eventually discover that their energy will be much cheaper than buying fools' fuel- oil, gas, and coal. These commodities are getting more and more costly. Solar and wind are free forever. Now that's a bargain.

How to make a small fortune in shale gas - Start with a large fortune!

For quite some time now, we have been propagandized with so called facts that state that shale derived gas is the solution to the energy needs of the world. Whenever, anybody tells you that anything is too good to be true, turn around and run as fast as you can away from them. Because IT IS TOO GOOD TO BE TRUE. Lots of good money is being poured into holes in the ground. The real story about shale gas is far different than the advertisements and the propagandized publicity releases. Analysts are beginning to expose the truths in this huge ruse. In fact, some analysts are calling the shale gas projects " just giant Ponzi schemes." Some gas wells take 7 years to just break even, and then stop producing. Many dry up way sooner, and don't even break even.

The New York Times has examined lots of emails and interviewed industry consultants and analysts who consistently state that the public perception of shale gas does not match reality. A retired geologist from the oil and gas industry wrote, " They want to bend light to hide the truth." The truth is that gas is not as cheap to extract from deep shale formations as the companies keep saying. In the emails reviewed by the NY Times, energy executives, industry lawyers, state geologists, and market analysts question whether companies are intentionally, and even illegally overstating the productivity of their wells, and the size of the gas reserves.

In addition to the many failed gas wells, many of the producing wells are running out of gas much faster than the predictions stated by company representatives.

In the June 26, 2011 NY Times article, Deborah Rogers, a member of the advisory committee of the Federal Reserve Bank of Dallas, stated that she started studying well data from shale companies in October 2009 and she found that the " math was not adding up." She stated that her research showed that the wells were petering out faster than expected.

The public is beginning to recognize that shale gas drilling is dangerous to public health.

The process is called hydraulic fracturing or hydrofracking. A single well can require ONE MILLION GALLONS OF WATER! This water becomes contaminated by the process. And we all know what happens when corporations have lots of dirty water to get rid of. Watch out for the water you drink or swim in. It can kill you. Not only will investors get hurt, but people living near these wells will get hurt too.

In July 2011 a new study by Mary Beth Adams, a US Forest Research researcher, appeared in the July issue of the Journal of Environmental Quality. The study took place on a quarter acre of land in the of the Fernow Experimental Forest in the Monohahela National Forest in the state of West Virginia. 75,000 gallons of fracking fluids which had been injected underground to free shale gas and then were returned to the earth's surface, were applied to an assigned plot over a 2 day period during June 2008. Here is what happens when Fracking fluid is dumped by drilling companies:
1) Within 2 days all of the ground plants were dead!
2) Within 10 days, leaves on trees began to turn brown. Within 2 years, more than half of the 150 trees were dead!
3) "Surface soil concentrations of sodium and chloride increased 50-fold as a result of the land application of hydrofracking fluids…"

PEER (Public Employees for Environmental Responsibility) Executive Director Jeff Ruch stated," The explosion of shale gas drilling in the East has the potential to turn large stretches of public land into lifeless moonscapes. This study suggests that these fluids should be treated as toxic waste."

What is the US government doing to protect? You? Or the Drillers?

So far the US government has been very lax in protecting the US public lands from the spreading of this toxic waste. And I might add that the US government is not too swift in solving the problems with nuclear power plants' waste either! The nuke waste has a lifetime of several thousand years, so I guess that gives some young terrorists plenty of time to figure out how to explode some of these sitting piles and buckets of fireworks! In a way it is a race of who will do the most damage – the drilling companies or the terrorists.

Will Obama cancel the Keystone XL Pipeline of tar sand oil that will carry tar sand oil from Canada to the US Gulf coast?

President Obama has the power to cancel this serious threat to several US states' environments. Secretary of State Hillary Clinton also could have stopped this environmental threat, but she signed on with the oil companies. It is now Obama's turn. This proposed pipeline has produced nationwide protests from people who are trying to get the US government out of the control of oil and gas corporations. We want safe energy. Will Obama help us or help the oil companies. The answer will come soon. Who do you think Obama will support?

If Al Gore were President, there would be no question . With Obama, there is. That is why I am trying to persuade Al Gore to run for US President. He can be trusted.

For the many people who want safe energy, I strongly recommend that you mobilize citizens to demand the banning of all hydrofracking, the closing of all nuclear power plants, and the banning of the Keystone XL tar sand pipeline. Large numbers of citizens can win, over large buckets of bribes to elected officials, if you work hard enough.

Another reason citizens should pay attention to these matters is because US federal and state officials are considering increasing the subsidies to these companies. This transfusion of tax money may end up draining down into empty holes in the ground. If you do not want this to happen, it is time to support the environmental organizations who are fighting hydrofracking. It is a fight worth getting into. And we must push and shove our government to stop wasting our tax dollars by diverting this money from safe energy sources to dirty oil, gas, and coal sources.

On June 28, 2011 a handful of US Congress persons and one US Senator responded to the NY Times expose of the gas industry, by calling for investigations of the gas industry by the US Securities and Exchange Commission, the Energy Information Administration, and the Government Accountability Office. This is not enough, but at least a few of the 500 plus elected federal officials in Washington responded. It will take far more than these few to stop the crooked path that US tax dollars follow to swerve into the wrong pockets.

Lies about Climate Change can cost millions of lives.

As you readers already know, or are learning now, the path to stopping Climate Change is littered with land mines of lies scattered by the millions of dollars paid to dishonest scientists by oil, gas, and coal industries, and the ultra rich Koch brothers who own oil, gas, and chemical companies. On June 28, 2011 the English newspaper, The Guardian, published an article about documents obtained by a Greenpeace investigation that disclosed how millions of dollars have been paid to scientists for several years to distort the information about Climate Change. The major contributors of this blood money are the Charles G Koch Foundation, the American Petroleum institute, Exxon Mobil, the Mobil Foundation, the Texaco Foundation, the Electric Power Research Institute.

Dr. Willie Soon, an astrophysicist, received $ 1 million in the past 10 years from the above oil interests. In 2003, Dr. Soon stated at a US Senate hearing that he had "not knowingly been hired by, nor employed by, nor received grants from any organization that had taken advocacy positions with respect to the Kyoto protocol or the UN Framework Convention on Climate Change."

In one email sent by Dr. Soon to 4 other scientists, he wrote, "Clearly the fourth assessment report may be too much for any one of us to tackle them all…But as a team, we may give it our best shot to try to anticipate and counter some of the chapters…"

He also wrote, " I hope we can…see what we can do to weaken the fourth assessment report."

Climate Change is a more serious threat to the survival of mankind than nuclear warfare. Yes, it is that bad! And it is gaining momentum while we all do nothing.

The world needs safe solar and wind energy, not the fools' fuels - dirty oil, gas, and coal. We all must transition to safe sources of energy as fast as we can. Every national government in the world must direct lots more money towards building the solar and wind industries.

Laws should be passed in every nation in the world. No nation should be allowed to shirk its responsibility to combat the gravest threat to humanity- Climate Change. We all are in this boat. We will sink or swim depending on 100% of nations cooperating in stopping this calamity from getting worse and worse.
This is a most important problem and it is not going away. It is getting worse each day we delay. The amount of money spent in clean up and conversion to

safer sources of energy are not only going to save our world from extinction, but will create many, many new industries that will employ millions of workers. This is good business. Ignoring this threat is not a consideration for any thinking citizen. We all are at risk. We must demand action NOW from our governments. The theme could be a simple sign. " Stop the Poisoning of our air and water!" "Arrest the polluters!"

No nation should be allowed to escape their responsibility to stop Climate Change!

Any nation that does not pass this legislation and does not enforce this legislation should be sanctioned by the UN and given a short period to comply. If the nation refuses to comply, they should be subject to penalties that could include a international boycott of their exports, plus a ban on tourists visiting their country. If the UN gains this power to enforce this needed propulsion of efforts to combat Climate Change, we will be saved from disaster.

This is the most serious threat to mankind, and everybody must act quickly to save us all. On July 21, 2011, Achim Steiner, director of the UN Environment Program, stated, " The scale of the natural disasters will increase exponentially. The signs of climate changing, not only is it happening, it is accelerating."

This is very frightening news, and we, the citizens must demand that our governments heed these warnings, and stop taking bribes to protect corporations from spending the money that is necessary to protect us all.

Let's put our thinking caps on. If executives of corporations refuse to stop their polluting our air, Climate Change will accelerate. The world will experience more and more severe storms. And people will be killed by these severe storms. These people were murdered by the criminal acts of those executives whose corporations could have easily afforded to buy the equipment to mitigate their pollution problems, and to switch to clean sources of energy. Their corporations would have made a little less gross profit during a short period of time. But, if nothing is done to stop Climate Change and the world's oceans begin to flood all of the cities located near water, the "Dump Cheap" corporations may be under water. I doubt if their water soaked annual financial statements will enable the "Dump Cheap" executives to cash in any stock options that year, or any year thereafter.
Climate Change carries many deadly threats to our planet. Storms are only one. The warming effects can bring diseases that kill.

Studies by 17 European marine institutions have just been publicized that the warming of our oceans is creating more Vibrio bacteria that can travel from fish to man and result in food poisoning, gastroenteritis, septicemia, and deadly cholera! Climate Change can upset the world's eco system so badly that parts of the world will become uninhabitable. The temperatures will become too hot or too cold to live in. Our food supplies will be threatened by the decrease in arable land to farm. Climate Change is decimating the planet we live on, and this is all we have. We can't move to another one and start all over.

We must treat our planet like we treat our automobiles. Avoid accidents. Give it regular maintenance. Treat it with great care. And don't let the adolescent CEOs wreck it.

Fossil fuel companies' lies exposed by Al Gore and Greenpeace

Another interesting thing happened in the month of June in 2011. Indeed, "June is bursting all over." Former US Vice President Al Gore had two different articles published. One was published by Rolling Stone magazine which is entitled , Climate of Denial: Can Science and the Truth Withstand the Merchants of Poison? He describes how the oil companies are financing pseudo scientists to manufacture doubt about Climate Change. So not only does Greenpeace, a leading environmental organization, prove this with documents, but a former Vice President of the USA confirms these dishonest attacks on the scientific findings about Climate Change.

Al Gore also refers to the 'buying elected officials wholesale with bribes that the politicians themselves have made "legal'. And he refers to the Supreme Court allowing this bribery to continue now in secret, by ruling against regulations that formerly required disclosure of the names of so called contributors. He also stated that there are 4 anti-climate lobbyists (not scientists) for every member of the US Senate and the House of Representatives. The oil, gas and coal companies are spending a lot of money to protect their sales of dirty fuels. All of their millions of dollars would be wasted if the USA had honest elected officials, who refused to accept bribes and threw the lobbyists out of their offices!

The science behind the findings on Climate Change has been endorsed by every national academy of science in every major country in the world!

It has been endorsed by every major professional scientific society related to the study of global warming, and by 98% of climate scientists throughout the world. In the latest authoritative study by 3,000 of the very best scientific experts in the world, the evidence was judged " unequivocal."

Al Gore also had an article published by the Associated Press, and written by Dina Cappielllo in June entitled, "Al Gore Blasts Obama on Climate Change for failing to take 'bold action". In this article, Gore is quoted as writing in his essay that," President Obama has never presented to the American people the magnitude of the climate crisis. He has not defended the science against the ongoing withering and dishonest attacks. Nor has he provided a presidential venue for the scientific community… to bring the reality of the science before the public."

Al Gore has issued a very pronounced critique of President Obama.

I agree 100% with these criticisms of Obama. I was a delegate for Obama in both the Colorado county and state conventions. I believed in what Obama said in his campaign speeches. He has failed to produce on so many issues that I have lost full confidence in him as a President. His lack of leadership and propensity to cave in to Republican demands is not what I voted for.

 He has had the power to stop a lot of bad legislation, but has chosen to simply smile and pen his ok on a lot of phony bills. He did not have to sign the credit card "reform" bill that lacked a cap on interest rates. The consequences of his not vetoing this phony bill is that millions of Americans are now paying usury interest rates that reach 30% and higher.

Obama should not have met with private insurance company lobbyists before the debate had even begun on the vitally needed makeover of US health insurance. He catered to these lobbyists' wildest dreams. He sided with Democratic Senator Max Baucus when the Senator called in Security people to prevent a group of doctors and nurses from presenting a real national healthcare plan at a public hearing! These doctors and nurses had travelled all over the USA and were enthusiastically cheered on by hopeful Americans that they would be allowed to help the public obtain a national health plan that would be affordable to all. Obama chose to never consider their plan.

Obama's plan is a fraction of what is needed by the 50 million people with no health insurance, and does not help the millions with health insurance that has such high deductibles that they cannot afford to enter a hospital. Obama seems a lot more interested in pleasing large corporations than protecting the public and the planet from their greedy and ruthless CEOs.

Yes, Al Gore is right. Obama has failed to throw his weight behind the real scientists who have been warning us that we must act now- before it is too late. Al Gore now realizes that he cannot stop Climate Change from the side lines, appealing to the consciences of the elected officials in Washington. He knows that a lot of them are accepting bribes to look the other way, while oil, gas, and coal companies continue to sell their dirty goods.

Al Gore for President!

After I read these two articles about Al Gore, I wrote an open letter to Al Gore, and sent it to the Washington Post newspaper to publish. I do not know if they published it, but I will tell you the contents of my letter to Gore.

Dear Al,
I agree with you that Obama has not fought against the oil, gas, and coal companies who are responsible for Climate Change. In fact, I personally, believe he feels more comfortable catering to the rich than fighting for the working people and the planet. He has had plenty of opportunities to join us. But he has consistently sided with the rich. Remember, he signed the bill that extended the huge tax giveaways to the richest people in the USA for another two years. With the country in hock for trillions of dollars, this weak kneed President allows the rich to pay less taxes, rather than more. I applaud you for all of the work you have done to stop Climate Change, but you must now recognize that you have failed to succeed, by working on the outside of this government.

I urge you to run for President. It is the only way that you can succeed in stopping Climate Change and protecting our planet for our children and grandchildren.

Once you become President, here is my wish list:
1) Push hard to expand solar and wind power so we can permanently stop dirtying the atmosphere with oil, gas, and coal.
2) Close all nuclear plants. Repeal all subsidies for nuclear plants. We have the legal grounds for this action. The nuclear power companies have consistently lied about their many violations of regulations. Fire all the people on the Nuclear Regulatory Commission, as they have acted only to protect the profits of the power companies. They have failed to protect the public. Start an investigation into whether bribery was involved in this cozy relationship.

3) Ban all contributions, personal as well as outside, in US elections. Destroy the cancer of democracy- corruption by bribery.
4) Criminalize pollution. Dump all the phony cap and trade schemes. Drop the word, "trade", and concentrate on creating laws that place caps on pollution. And I mean steel caps, not loopholes to get around the laws. Put executives in jail if they deliberately pollute. Change semantics from pollute to poison.
5) Ban sales of gasoline driven cars. Push sales of electric cars.
6) Ban use of food for fuel. Allow bio fuels from plant waste, such as stalks, weeds, etc. Outlaw use of corn, etc to be used for fuel. This practice of corn for fuel has caused starvation in poor countries, and ultimately will wreck our distribution of food in the USA, as well as around the world. Repeal any subsidies for food as fuel.
7) Use your voice as President to persuade people in all countries to switch to a Vegan diet. Using land to feed animals is causing 30% of atmospheric pollution. People will live longer and enjoy healthier lives by not eating meat and dairy diets. The facts from the China Study are overwhelming.

The world needs better leaders. America needs you.

Howard Greenebaum author of "Free Elections ???" a book published in 1990 about electoral reform.

(I have taken literary license to elongate my 200 word limited letter to the editor. Please excuse, but if the letter to the editor does not get published, perhaps this extended version may yet reach the eyes of respected leaders of my country, and of your countries.)

How your tax dollars have become gifts

I would like to expand your knowledge of how governmental handouts of subsidies gets corrupted. Government officials have many ways to help their rich "contributors." One way is to place tariffs on imports, so their "friends" businesses can be spared the stress of competing with foreign made products. A second and more direct fashion is to legislate the government to send checks (subsidies) to special people for special reasons. Let's take a look at the US farm bill.

This spicy bit of legislation sends billions of tax dollars, masked as subsidies, for the largest 5 commodity crops in the USA, corn, cotton, rice, wheat, and soybeans. Since 1995, the largest agricultural enterprises received 74% of all "farm" subsidies!) 62% of real farmers did not receive any subsidies.

While President Obama's wife parades around making speeches about improving the diet of Americans, her husband has allowed the farm bill to almost totally neglect financial help to farmers raising fruit and vegetables! In 2012, their meager financial assistance may shrink to zero.

The 2008 farm bill passed a rule that subsidies should only go to "actively engaged" farmers. This rule has been ignored. 90,000 checks have been sent to wealthy investors and absentee land owners in 350 American cities in 2010!

The subsidies also reward farmers for diverting crops from organically grown food to fertilizer and pesticide intensive crops. This is a mighty help to manufacturers of fertilizer and pesticide products, but is harmful to our environment and to our drinking water, and to your health.

The bio fuel screw up

Corn is America's largest crop. The price of corn has doubled in one year! 40% of corn goes toward feeding animals that many people eat. Another 40% is now going toward making ethanol. We now can see why the price of corn has doubled. The corn business attracts $11 billion in tax payer subsidies. If we all converted to a Vegan diet, we could save 40% of the corn, that is now eaten by animals that we would no longer eat. If we stopped diverting another 40% of our corn crop to ethanol, we would have more corn at a lower price to eat, and to share with the world.

Ethanol consumes more energy than it produces!

Much of the hype of ethanol has not been proven to be true. Making corn ethanol also consumes huge quantities of water, which is something that no nation can spare. By being able to sell corn again at an affordable price, millions of consumers in America, and around the world, would benefit. It is time that governments all over the world stop thinking within a box.

Decisions in one nation affect citizens in other nations.

As an example, East Africa is now suffering from the worst drought in 60 years! People in many areas of Somalia are suffering from famine, and thousands are leaving their homes in search for food and water.
If each nation took into consideration the problems of their neighbors across some borders, food and water shortages could be rapidly mitigated. I believe it is time to extend our caring beyond the walls of our homes. We all can contribute by opening our minds to solving the problems of others less affluent than us. A rethink of tariffs, subsidies, and planting of crops might

bring more business to the producers, and save lives of people caught up in natural disasters.

Certainly there is going to be no shortages of "natural" disasters with rapidly accelerating Climate Change.

At a teleconference of scientists in June 2011, they issued a statement that " the global temperatures have been warmer than the 20th century's average every month for more than 25 years!"

" The indicators show unequivocally the world continues to warm", stated Thomas Karl, director of the National Climatic Data Centre, in their 2010 State of the Climate report.

Peter Thorne of the Co-operative Institute for Climate and Satellites at North Carolina State University stated, " There is a clear and unmistakable signal from the top of the atmosphere to the oceans' depths."

Why our oceans are so important to our survival

It is essential that we all recognize the connections of oceans to our very survival. And I am not referring to the real threat to the seafood industry. I am writing about the oxygen that keeps us alive. Photosynthetic organisms in the oceans yield most of the oxygen in the atmosphere! The decrease in oxygen creates hypoxia. And that ain't good. In short, it means we cannot exist without plenty of clean air, and our air sources are under attack by pollutants. To protect our children and grand children, we must stop the polluters who are sending huge amounts of lethal carbon dioxide into our atmosphere, and into our oceans. This bad behaviour affects our planctary chemistry, which keeps us alive.

Yes, our very lives depend on a healthy and clean ocean.

And, unfortunately, we are doing a terrible job of protecting our oceans. Our oceans absorb one third of the carbon dioxide emitted to the atmosphere from the polluting fuels of oil, gas, and coal. This is not good. The CO2 then dissolves in the waters, and decreases the pH of the water. This process is called acidification of the ocean. This process is taking pace at a speed never before recorded in history. These changes have not been experienced in millions of years! The volumes of pollution are at least tripling, and the pace is accelerating at a pace that is terrifying to all the honest scientists that are observing this ongoing disaster.

The greed of the fishing industry is rapidly destroying the entire marine ecosystem.

They are taking out far more fish than the ecosystem can replace. This is disrupting the food chains throughout the oceans. It is responsible for causing an imbalance of all the creations in the oceans. The theme, " get rich quick" is not only prevalent on New York's Wall Street, but is in practice everywhere fish swim.

The obvious solution is to stop the mad race to oblivion. We all must learn to share and be sensitive to the effects of our conduct. We must learn to live by "sanctity of conduct." (to be free from sin). It is sinful to destroy the foundation of our means to survival. Over fishing cannot be tolerated. They are killing all of the fish. It is that simple.

The ocean has also been used as a dumping ground.

This " out of sight, out of mind" thinking is not only stupid, but it is becoming very dangerous to us all. Why? Let me explain. In the central North Pacific ocean lies a man made <u>continent sized</u> glob of trash. This mass of junk is over 100 feet (30 meters) deep from its floating surface to its filthy bottom. And its size is truly larger than the whole USA! It even has a name, "Pacific Trash Vortex". Its location is 135-155 degrees W by 35-42 degrees N. The UN environmental report tagged this colossal floating mass as the "world's new toxic time bomb." Why?

There are tons and tons of plastics in this mass. Plastics do not biodegrade. But, unfortunately, they do photo degrade. Sunlight breaks plastics down to smaller and smaller bits and pieces which eventually become molecules of plastic. Unfortunately, these molecules are invisible, and are too tough for creatures to safely digest. These new particles accumulate with many very toxic elements that then travel from fish to mankind. They include DDT, PCB, and nonylphenols (oily toxics).

Ultimately, humans will absorb some of these demons through our hormone receptors.

The results of getting these things into our bodies are bad. It will result in lower sperm counts, and in imbalanced gender numbers. This imbalance of genders can ultimately lead to the extinction of the human race! That's all.

Quite a price to pay for tossing our trash into the oceans. Since we all are guilty of dirtying our oceans, we all must stop it - at once! And we might even consider limiting the manufacturing of plastics, or outright banning the use of plastics. They are that dangerous, to the future of mankind.

There are many facets to the protection of our planet.

But, as you can see, they all must be addressed, for mankind to exist. We cannot pride ourselves on our ignorance. We must educate ourselves, in order to be able to protect our families from the results of past abuses of our environment by so many. Ignorance, in a computer world, is no excuse or alibi. We are all living here, and must learn to be responsible residents.

So, I will do my best to bring these problems to your attention, and, of course, offer some solutions. If we all know more, we can do more. And if you are feeling overwhelmed by this myriad of problems, just close your eyes and imagine what it would be like to be blind. That's worse than my book giving you a little headache. No, you do not have to solve all of these problems by yourself.

You must not close your eyes and your mind to the many threats to mankind.

The answer to all of these problems is for you and you and you to help open the eyes and minds of others, so we can all mobilize and conquer. As I made a list for this book, others can make their lists and start organizing people so these problems will be fixed quickly. Remember, there are common denominators that are responsible for many, many problems. For example, bribery by a few to another few in power can pay for blinders over the eyes of our so called representatives.

Most of these diverse problems have been exposed before, in open, public hearings by your and my governments. The common denominator at these hearings was bribery. There is not much sense in airing problems to a bunch of crooks who only care about themselves and their next elections. Corruption can be stamped out. It will not be thrown out by the people receiving the bribes. They are contaminated by cash. They must be thrown out of both political parties by you voters.

Remember the title of this chapter, "we will never get a clean environment with a dirty government." Many governments have been tossed out because of corruption by people like you and you. Signing petitions online won't buy it. You have got to get mad and get involved. Crooked politicians thrive on the apathy of voters.

We must elect people who care for the environment more than their reelection!

Recently, on June 22, 2011, the Center for Biological Diversity notified the US EPA (Environmental Protection Agency) that it was going to file a lawsuit for its failure to try to reduce black carbon, a powerful global warming pollutant. As with many US federal agencies, they have a tendency to act much too late, which enables problems to grow rather than be reduced in intensity. Black carbon comes from the incomplete combustion of fossil fuels, oil, gas, and coal. These particles enter the atmosphere and cause it to warm. They also fall on ice and snow, and by their dark color attract and absorb heat and then, of course, speed up the melting. This acceleration of natural melting of ice and snow is causing Climate Change.

The EPA needs to do their job a lot faster and a lot better to help stop Climate Change. They must do everything that they can to protect the sea ice and glaciers under the US Clean Water Act. Unfortunately, the US Republican Party is more interested in protecting the profits of corporations than protecting the health of American citizens. In fact, they are trying to cut funds to the EPA , and are also trying to weaken the regulations under the Clean Water Act and the Clean Air Act. (They also are trying to privatize all public healthcare programs.) The black carbon causes hundreds of thousands of deaths each year in the USA. Once more it is so necessary for voters to connect the dots, in order to vote for their interests. Too many voters fail to recognize these facts, and end up voting against their own interests. Let that be a lesson to learn around the world!

Water, water everywhere- but none that I can afford!

This chapter is dedicated to protection of the planet. No single element is more important for the survival of mankind, animals, or plant life than water. A person can live far longer without food than without water. There are a lot of movements by rich investors to privatize access to water.
We, the citizens of this world, must be alert to these greed driven individuals and corporations. Every human being must be granted several rights pertaining to water. Basically they are:
1) A human must have access to affordable water, in order to prevent death by dehydration.
2) A human must have the right to obtain water that is safe from disease and pollution.

3) A human must have the right to obtain water this is safe to use for cooking food.

4) A human must have the right to obtain water in order to maintain hygiene.

The population of the world in 2011 is 7 billion. In 50 years the population will grow to 10.5 billion. We must do our planning now so that each person can have access to water for survival.

Today, 1.1 billion people lack access to safe drinking water. 2.6 billion people lack adequate water for sanitation. And 1.5 million children die each year from water borne diseases. So we can see that we have done a terrible job for the existing 7 billion. If we do not make changes, 50 years from now will bring worldwide calamity.

All of these facts and numbers seem overwhelming, don't they? Well, be patient and let me show you how to make a big problem simple to understand and simple to solve.

Fortunately there is much we can do now. Let us look at these simple numbers below:

1 kg of wheat requires 1,000 liters of water

1 kg of rice requires   1,400 liters of water

1 kg of meat requires 13,000 liters of water

One simple solution, with many benefits to you – The Vegan Diet.

66% of water today is used for irrigation. If we all converted to the Vegan diet of fruit, vegetables, and grains. (no meat or dairy) we would not be wasting 13,000 liters of water to produce 1 kg of meat! We would free the land to grow more vegetables, fruit, and grains. The Vegan diet not only is the solution for providing more water, but it reduces 30% of the air borne air pollution. And the diet is cheaper than a meat and dairy diet! So more people can afford it.
And by escaping from a meat diet, you will be free from many life threatening diseases- heart disease, cancer, and diabetes. So people will be stronger, healthier, and live longer.

The myth that you need to eat meat to get protein is simply untrue.

In fact the world famous China Study proved that meat protein fuels the growth of cancer, while the Vegan diet starves the growth of cancer. Protein is found in all forms of food, and you can easily get a list of foods with the content of protein in each item. Many of the top athletes in the world are Vegans, so strength is a selling point, not a detriment.

The Vegan diet also sheds lots of pounds from your body in a natural way so the pounds are lost forever. This is the diet that humans were meant to eat. Remember, the strongest animals in the world are Vegans. Elephants and horses are Vegans! The tallest animal in the world is a Vegan, the giraffe! So, we have in front of our eyes, a common denominator that covers poverty, bad health, and combating Climate Change.! And all you and you and you have to do is convert your diet to a safe diet called Vegan.

I will give you more facts on the Vegan diet in another chapter in this book. So hang in there, you will be learning how to live longer and healthier while you are providing more water to the fast growing population of the world.

Conservation of water is a must

The other 34% of water is used by households. Once again, there are excellent options here also. Each house should be refitted with a second pipe for conservation purposes. After using water for cooking, washing, and for sanitation , this water should be sent out the new pipe into a recycling device that prepares it for external use. This water then can be reused for washing windows and cars, and for irrigating gardens and lawns. We also can plant different types of plants that require less water, and still provide beautification.

Another possibility should be considered for sanitation. For some time now cities have depended on collecting human waste matter through an elaborate system of piping, and directing it to waste treatment plants. This centralized waste treatment program then is the final receptor for millions of liters of dirty water. Most houses have some lawn around them. We might consider installing waterless toilets in homes and providing a septic tank on each property. Without water, the tank would not have to be that large. There also might be available some sort of home compost system that can convert the human waste into fertilizer for the gardens. These alternatives to centralized waste systems can save huge amounts of water.

Centralized sewerage systems- are they necessary?

In the late 1980s I attended a city council meeting in San Diego, California about the pollution problems of their centralized sewerage system. Frequent sightings of floating human waste had caused frequent closings of the public beaches around this beautiful city. Their former Republican mayor, Pete Wilson, had opposed upgrading this system. The system had a large steel pipe jutting out into the ocean releasing tons of pollution and toxic materials. If the mayor had approved the upgrading of the system, the federal Clean Water Act would have contributed at least 90% of the funding for this upgrade. By the time this city council hearing took place, the Clean Water Act's funding was no longer available.

However, I spoke to the City Council and convinced them to vote 8 to 1 to abandon their waiver from the Clean Water Act that Wilson had obtained for this faulty system. For the next several years after this city council meeting, San Diego politicians fought over how to keep their beaches clean and at the same time comply with the regulations of the US Clean Water Act. They could not agree to upgrade their system, so they compromised and simply extended the existing pipe farther out from the beaches! Sad but true.

Centralized sewerage systems are very, very expensive and there are alternatives to dumping into our oceans. Waterless toilets is one option. I am sure if the world stopped paying our smartest scientists and engineers to design weapons of war, and redirected their efforts toward peaceful projects, we would soon have many options available.

And another very important advantage to this conversion from centralized sewerage systems would be huge decreases in emptying the treated waste water into oceans. Oceans certainly do not need any more dumping than is already happening. In fact, we could decrease a considerable amount of dumping by using waterless toilets, thereby adding protection to our oceans. We have already learned that oceans are not for dumping. They are a fragile member of our ecosystem that needs a lot better care than it has been receiving up to now. With the growing population of our world, we all must open our minds to new ideas. Our intellects must get popping to address the myriad of problems facing us. If we inject integrity into our governments by throwing out the lobbyists and the bribed elected officials, we can produce a safe, healthier, happier, and more prosperous world.

As we continue to learn how so many things are causing Climate Change, we must never stop paying attention to the choices being offered by our governments. We all know that money manages to creep into the pockets of politicians. And we also know that politicians tend to bend the truth at times. In fact, if they get some really good bribes, they tend to distribute bountiful lies.

Obama and the planet.

And this leads me to pay attention to US President Barack Obama and his behaviour towards our environment. Obama continues to say "clean coal", and "safe nuclear" power-which are oxymorons. Oxymorons are two words that are opposites, but morons and politicians say them together, as if they were twins. Obama has been a nice guy to a lot of people. Unfortunately, these people happen to be the guys who own coal mines, sell nuclear power plants, and run big banks.

He has pushed nuclear power, even after the nuclear melt downs in Japan! He has been instrumental in the offering of very liberal subsidies worth billions of dollars, to nuclear power companies. And this subsidizing of nuclear power plants must stop! Nuclear power is much too dangerous for the world to gamble on. The lies coming from the power companies are fodder for trash cans. They definitely cannot be trusted.

Obama can read. Right. He even went to college. Right. So why is he favoring dangerous and dirty sources of our energy? I have an idea why. What do you think?

Nuclear power is almost as dangerous as allowing children to play with matches.

The materials that nuclear reactors are made of, are brittle. Intense heat breaks down brittle materials. 75% of US nuclear plants are victims of corrosion. This causes leaks of radioactive material that can kill people. Radioactive tritium has leaked from these so called "safe" plants all over the USA, and has been found in groundwater near corroded pipes buried underground! And these threats to US drinking water have been escalating, according to an Associated Press investigation released in June 2011.

The super heat in nuclear reactors eventually causes the parts to crack and split. I attended a public hearing in North Carolina in 1985 about a crack in the nuclear reactor at North Brunswich. They rolled out a model of what they planned to do to fix the crack. There were executives from the top power company and executives from the NRC at the hearing. They all applauded the recommendation of installing a steel band around the reactor. They began to rise from their seats and get ready to leave the stage, when I exclaimed, " This is a cover up." Evidently that word sent chills down their conforming backs, because everyone on the stage returned to their seats and were very quiet. I stated that, the model was similar to attaching a Band-Aid around a cracked tea cup."

I also reminded the executives that this plant had been victimized by the installer who had been found guilty of installing counterfeit bolts in the walls that did not contribute to the safety of the structure. The power company had to spend a great deal of money to correct the many deliberate failures to build the nuclear plant according to the specs. I also reminded the executives that the North Brunswich plants were sitting right next to an earthquake fault!

Despite my warnings, these two troubled plants have had their licenses extended by the NRC and are still operating in North Carolina today! These two nuclear plants are the exact same model as the ones in Japan that just suffered meltdowns! This part of North Carolina also has been a favorite target for hurricanes throughout history! I believe the people of North Carolina need to rise up and demand these sitting time bombs be closed before it is too late.

There are at least 23 of this model reactors sitting around cities in the USA today. I strongly encourage people in every nation to rise and demand the closings of all nuclear power plants before Mother Nature closes them for us, and spews radioactive materials around the world killing millions of people with the resulting cancers.

The US Nuclear Regulatory Commission (NRC) has had a very cozy relationship with power companies who operate nuclear power plants.

The US plants were supposed to have a lifetime of 40 years. However, the NRC has continued to extend the licenses on these old and cracking nuke plants for years and years after their deadlines for safety. The NRC has continued to bend the safety requirements and ignore the safety violations of most of these sitting time bombs.

So what happened in Japan can, indeed, happen in any country, France included. In June 2011, French politicians were harping that their nuke plants were safe. Two weeks later a French nuke plant suffered an explosion! This happened 2 days after French inspectors had found 32 safety violations at this plant!
There are other nuclear power plants sitting next to earthquake fault lines. On August 24, 2011 a 5.9 magnitude earthquake occurred 90 miles from the US capitol in Virginia. This earthquake was felt in several states up and down the East Coast of the USA. The earthquake was on a fault line that was right by

two nuclear power plants! The electricity of the plant was affected. Fortunately the backup generators flipped on and the plants were saved.

However, the huge accumulations of nuclear waste was not protected by any backup generators. These accumulations of nuclear waste sitting by nuclear power plants around the USA are not protected by backup generators! These also may be labeled, " sitting time bombs." There is nothing safe about nuclear waste.

Why does the NRC ignore public safety and favor the power companies?

I believe this is a very good question. I believe that every member of the NRC should be investigated. I believe the investigation should look at the NRC members' bank accounts, stock share holdings, safety deposit boxes in banks, and every financial paper belonging to these people, who have acted so benevolent toward the power companies owning nuke plants.

A great number of US federal agencies have abandoned their role of protecting the public and have entered into collusion with the 'Special interests that they are supposed to be regulating. I believe the public should learn why they are being exposed to lurking dangers from crumbling nuke plants by an agency that has done far too many favors for the nuke industry. Many of these nuke plants are very near cities with large populations. If one of these nuke plants has a meltdown, millions of people will be exposed to radioactivity such as the Japanese citizens are now experiencing due to their nuke plant meltdowns.

And the media has failed us too.

The media has been parroting statements from their advertisers, and from dishonest scientists, that there is no danger from small amounts of radioactivity. This is not the truth!

In 2000 the UN Scientific Committee on the Effects of Atomic Radiation released a statement that said there is no safe level of exposure to radiation.

In 2001 The US National Council on Radiation Protection and Measurements released a similar statement.
In 2004 the United States Research Council cautioned the world with the same words.

In 2006 the US National Academy of Sciences concluded a report with these words," there is a linear, no-threshold dose-response relationship between exposure to ionizing radiation and the development of cancers in humans."

With all of these prestigious scientific organizations warning us of ANY EXPOSURE to radiation, it is time for us to act. We know that nothing is perfect. Consequently, we must conclude that nuclear power plants will eventually break down and leak radioactivity into the air. We also know that winds blow radioactivity thousands of miles. The only way to stop this exposure to radioactivity is to close all nuclear power plants as soon as possible. The race to safe energy is on.

And if you are still not convinced, here is some more information to ponder. Many scientists have now stated that Chernobyl "has already contributed to hundreds of thousands of excess deaths." This is bad news for the Japanese people who are facing potentially more radiation exposure than Chernobyl.

Why we will never know how dangerous the Japanese meltdowns were to us.

After a lot of spin talk from the Japanese government and the Tokyo Electric Power Co., they have finally admitted that not one, not two, but THREE NUCLEAR REACTORS MELTED DOWN! At the same time that radioactivity was being reported by scientists across the United States, from California to Vermont, something curious happened. The US Government shut down the US reporting of this travelling radioactivity. Americans were no longer able to read how much radioactivity was arriving from Japan! This is a serious symptom of how corrupt the US government has become. And how corrupt the media has become.

Once more governments and media have chosen to protect the profits of corporations over protecting the public. And President Obama continues to play Nero's fiddle while Americans breathe poisoned air from failing nuclear plants, and we all are becoming besieged by so called "natural disasters" caused by Climate Change.

Climate Change is not a natural disaster. It is caused by humans abusing our planet. So it is time to be more discretionary when we label a severe storm that is killing people and destroying their homes. These increases of destruction and mayhem are not from natural causes. They are from using the wrong fuels. They are from pumping dangerous gases into our atmosphere. They are from not paying attention to the behaviour of big corporations.

Nuclear waste here. Nuclear waste there. Nuclear waste everywhere!

Besides the real concerns of meltdowns of nuclear power plants around the world, we must never forget the ever dangerous radioactive waste stored around the world. This is a story that has been buried for too long a time. In 2002 the US Congress approved using the Yucca Mountain in the US state of Nevada as a place to store high level nuclear reactor waste. It is now 9 years later and 9 years full of debate about the Yucca Mt. nuclear waste location.

On March 3, 2010 the US Department of Energy filed a motion with the NRC to withdraw the license application for a nuclear waste repository at Yucca Mt.! Funding for the Yucca nuclear waste program was completely removed from the 2011 US federal budget. Does that mean that there is no need for storage for nuclear waste? Not exactly.

There are 30 million spend nuclear fuel rods unsafely stored along side of Nuclear power plants sitting near large cities in the USA. The whole discussion about nuclear waste got buried by the promoters of new nuke plants, but this actual nuclear waste has never been buried at the only selected site in the USA!

" Unprotected and crowded spent nuclear fuel rods pose an unacceptable threat to the public", stated Robert Alvarez. Alvarez is the senior scholar for nuclear policy at the Institute for Policy Studies. Before working for this Institute, he served at the Department of Energy as Senior Policy Advisor to the Secretary and Deputy Assistant Secretary for National Security and the Environment in the US government. While working there, he was awarded two secretarial gold medals. His employment also included serving as a Senior Investigator for the US Senate Committee on Governmental Affairs. Needless to say, this man knows what he is talking about.

Alvarez explained that spent nuclear rods are now stored in pools of water relying on a continual flow of electricity to keep the pools cool. The metal tubes that contain the nuclear fuel are as thin as a credit card! If this thin tubing cracks or breaks, it will release deadly radioactivity into the air. Alvarez gave an example of how deadly these spent rods are.

" If a motorcyclist rode by at 60 mph a foot away from the rods, he would be killed by the effects of that fleeting exposure!" "If the pool of water leaks, and drains the water from the pool, it can lead to a " catastrophic radioactive fire that spews toxins."

These pools of water containing spent nuclear rods are vulnerable to terrorist attacks, earthquakes, or even a prolonged electricity blackout! And the NRC, in their ever sincere efforts to always protect the profits of nuclear power companies, has not required the nuclear plants to install back up power equipment to prevent a catastrophe- or two-or more!

In the past, regulations were created by honest elected officials who cared for people and our planet. Then along came an ex -movie star named Ronald Reagan whose slogan was , "Let's get the government off our backs." Now Reagan was a very likeable movie actor. And everybody loved him. Unfortunately we did not understand what he was doing. You see, every regulation was created because some big company was cheating somebody or exposing their workers to life threatening conditions. These regulations have saved millions of people's lives.

Reagan was engaged in a pay back to his big corporation contributors. For if there is one thing that all corporations hate, it is regulations! The CEOs of corporations want to become rich and richer. They achieve this by firing good workers, and replacing them with low wage workers in poor countries whose governments also enjoy receiving bribes. These CEOs not only cut their labor costs, but they escape the regulations that protect the people living near their polluting factories, and escape the regulations that protect the workers inside their factories. This is a win - win for corporate profits. It is also a lose - lose for the exploited workers, and the neighbors of the dirty factories in other countries.

The coziness of elected officials to corporations is disgusting. In the US government, the Republicans are calling for the repeal of environmental protection regulations. They also are calling for cuts in the funding of environmental regulatory agencies.

The coziness of regulators to corporations is very dangerous, and it must stop now.

Barack Obama cannot be counted on to close US nuke plants.

America needs a President who will protect the public and not cater to the rich. It is that simple. Nation after nation around the world are now beginning to close all of their nuke plants. The resistance to these closings equals the amounts of bribes being distributed to our so called representatives in our governments. I suggest that voters in all countries ask all candidates for public office to sign pledges that they will vote to close all nuke plants in their countries, and if they later ignore this pledge, that the public will have the legislated power to recall these liars from office.

Nuclear power plants are too dangerous to be tolerated. It is another reason why we must prioritize production of safe solar and wind power to the top of the government's list for infrastructure building. We all must rid our countries from dangerous nuclear power plants, and of course, from the equally dangerous causes of Climate Change: oil, gas, and coal.

Every nation must legislate a separation of corporation from state.

The many rich corporations who have distributed bribes to our governments so they can continue to make more billions of dollars in profits must be confronted and stopped from corrupting our governments and the decision making by these bribed officials. Their claims that they cannot afford to operate cleanly are lies. Not all corporations are operating recklessly. It is time that we learn the names of corporations that do not bribe our officials and learn the names of corporations who have already converted to solar and wind power for their energy. These companies need to be rewarded with our business.

Crooked CEOs will never be happy until they all are billionaires.

The cost of their lust for excessive profits is your wages, your job, the health of your family, and the future for your children. Hoarding billionaires and hoarding multi- millionaires are the problem. Everybody must learn to share more, so we all can live safely and all enjoy a piece of prosperity.

The truth is that corporations making quality products will make profits.

Excessive profits come at the cost of safety to all creatures dwelling on our planet. We need to learn how to read financial statements of corporations. How much profit does a corporation need? What do corporations do with these profits? The more we learn how the present imbalanced economy is working only for a few , the quicker we will begin to learn how to change it so more people can be safe, healthy, happy, and prosperous. There is a lot more there to share, than the CEOs want you to learn.

Beware of smears about this book. Truths hurt the liars.

Greedy and ruthless people will try and persuade people to not read this book. They are afraid of your learning the truth. They are afraid of losing a few million dollars to taxes. They are afraid they will have to sell some of the houses they own around the world.

Remember during the presidential campaign between Obama and John McCain when a reporter asked McCain how many houses he owned? McCain did not even know how many houses he owned! That is excessive wealth. That is greedy hoarding. That is what an imbalanced economy produces. That is what we need to fix.

People will call me a communist.

These people are desperate to keep the world as it is. But we all must defend a book with new ideas that will protect our jobs, our children's futures, our planet , and provide more prosperity to all.

I am not a communist, and have never been a communist. I have been an international businessman all of my life. I am a thinker and a problem solver. I believe that we all can do a lot better when we have opened our minds to new ideas.   I have written this book to save the planet, and to stop the exploitation of workers in all nations.

Silence will not do. If you believe what I have written, please defend it.

The 2% of the population that owns so much of the wealth of the world does not want you to be exposed to the truths in this book. They will call me names and hope you believe these lies. Remember, many of these people have been attending meetings held by the Koch brothers who are spending millions of dollars spreading lies about Climate Change, and many other truths. Many rich corporations have contributed to the phony good named, but bad acting lie factories funded by the Kochs of industry.

Who do you now believe? Don't keep it a secret. Tell your friends about this book and encourage them to read it. We, the thinkers, must help others open their minds to ideas that can help the other 98% of the population. I think the 2% has helped itself pretty well. Don't you?

As you can tell by this chapter, I have spent a lot of my lifetime studying environmental papers, and trying to protect our environment. I would like to conclude this chapter with some good news about cities and nations working to protect our planet.

Especially the less developed nations, who have pledged to cut their emissions by far more than the industrialized nations. Many of the less developed nations are ahead of the industrialized nations in building safe energy programs for their futures. By 2020, the emission reductions by China, India, South Africa , and Brazil could be larger than the 7 largest industrialized nations, combined.

I suggest that we may assume that the governments of China, India, South Africa, and Brazil might be less corrupt than those of the 7 industrialized nations. How else can you explain the difference? Certainly all governments have the same knowledge of threatening Climate Change. Why would your government be hanging back on cutting life threatening emissions unless your elected officials were being bribed to protect the profits of their "friends", rather than protecting the lives of the people in your country?

The English have done an excellent job of insulating over 80% of older homes in their country! They are now trying to drum up business in the USA, but America has not received the support that the Brits received. The green industries are thriving in Britain due to these incentives.

This lack of government support for developing green alternatives, and providing incentives to conserve energy is costing the USA dearly.

The country is losing the many opportunities to expand US industries and provide jobs and safety to the nation. Why has this happened? The media claims that government officials are still not convinced that Climate Change is real! I wonder if the media really believes these phony alibis. Or perhaps, some of the media still believes that the earth is flat.

By now every reader of this book knows the real reason why elected officials in the US have not acted to protect the people from Climate Change. One word spells it out- BRIBERY! The US government is paralyzed by bribes from corporations who want to keep selling oil, gas, and coal until the last drop, fume, and grain are left to sell. These CEOs are frozen in their lust for gold, and continue to spin lies to the lazy and corrupt media that distributes these lies to the apathetic US public.

Meanwhile Europe, Asia, and South America are enjoying wonderful growth in their green industries.

They are racing ahead, while the bribed American government is still sitting at the starting gate. This is a disgrace, and is hurting millions of unemployed workers in the USA. This corruption in US government has cost the nation billions of dollars in business, and inflicted untold misery on struggling US families.

Dr. Arun Majumda, senior adviser to US Energy Secretary Steven Chu, stated, "We cannot do more without the support of Congress. We need better low cost financing methods to bring companies into the market, as well as stricter energy efficient standards to stimulate customer demand. We want this ecosystem to grow and thrive like I.T. and biotechnology....We are falling behind already."

Some American cities and states are trying.

 Even without the support of the federal government. California has been way out front. The city of Chicago has been very busy preparing for Climate Change. Chicago is repaving alleys, streets, and parking lots with materials that allow water to seep through to the ground underneath. They began a very diversified program way back in 2006. They stated that the alleys, streets, and parking lots account for 40% of ground cover, and attracted heat and trapped water. Their ideas could be used in cities all over the world. I am sure they would share their information with any reader who is interested in this excellent program. Chicago has also switched from planting trees that are susceptible to diseases caused by excessive heat –to trees that are tough, like swamp white oaks and bald cypress.

Cities all over the world should create a central information center where they all can share these type ideas that will help the public cope with the effects of Climate Change.

And for the last doubting Thomas reading this book, I present this gem of information about Climate Change.

As we all know some of the smartest people in the world work for insurance companies. They study all types of risk situations and then calculate the odds on claims from these situations, affecting the pricing of premiums. Here is what the reinsurance giant Swiss Re's head of sustainable development for the Americas, Mark D. Way, said," Society needs to reduce its vulnerability to climate risks, and as long as they remain manageable , they remain insurable, which is our interest as well."

Insurance companies are urging communities to adapt or pay higher premiums or not be able to find insurance! They know that Climate Change is a huge threat to us all, and are issuing these dire warnings.

With these summaries of successes and failures, I close this chapter on the theme that I started this chapter with, " We will never get clean environments with dirty governments." I doubt if my country, the USA , is the only nation suffering from a corrupt government. I will devote the last chapter in this book to stories about corruption, and my recommendations on how to stamp out this cancer of ailing governments.

HUMAN RIGHTS

"My God is better than your God - Bang!
My skin is better than your skin - No job!
My country is better than your country - Boom!
You look bad. Get 'em, guys! - Lynch mob!"......*H. Greenebaum*

Each chapter in this book attempts to put the pieces of the puzzle together, of how to make each country in the world a nice place to live and bring up your family. Nobody said it would be easy, but if you are serious in trying to help others bring peace and justice to the world, you need to learn all the facets to polish, on this gem of a goal.

The history of man includes many, many religions, dating back thousands of years.

Some religions worshipped several gods. Some chose only one god. Today, there is a long list of religions prevalent around the world. To give you a perspective, I will list just a few of the different beliefs, with the approximate population of each.

Christians	2.0 billion
Islam	1.4 billion
Hinduism	1.4 billion
Buddhism	1.0 billion

Non-believers	1.1 billion
African traditional	100 million
Judaism	14 million
Unitarians	800 thousand

The history of so many religions, unfortunately, has been one of intolerance for "the other religions."

Terrible wars have been fought over whose religion is the better. These wars are still being waged in several regions in the world today. It is time that all religious leaders met and discussed how to stamp out the rampant intolerance of each others' beliefs. It is my understanding that all religions are supposed to teach its believers to love mankind. Then, why are so many people walking out of their houses of worship, and then going to war against each other?

And speaking of love for thy neighbor, how about love for thy wife?

Too many religions teach males to treat their wives as possessions that they are allowed to dominate and abuse. Females in several religions are not allowed the same human rights that their husbands possess. Is it not about time for females to possess the same human rights as males? Once more, I believe religious leaders need to address this terrible situation for females around the world. And if religious leaders are not up to the job, we, the citizens, must demand that our governments grant females equal rights.

If a male does not believe this is a problem, I suggest that he put on a dress and lip stick and try and drive a car in Saudi Arabia. The last woman who tried to drive a car there ended up in jail! And that is a minor problem for females to overcome in many nations. The founders of the US Constitution inserted many wise requirements. One was the separation of church/religion from state. I believe that every nation must have a national constitution that separates church from state, so no one religion can take control of the government and implement the rules of their religion over an entire populace. As an example, what right does the Taliban have to ban education, employment, freedom of movement, etc. from the entire female population of a nation ruled by Taliban religious leaders?

By allowing religious leaders to control a nation's government, all other religions in this nation are put at grave risk. Intolerance of others' beliefs will evolve into a tyranny of minds by the ruling religious leaders.

After the US coup d'état of Iran's democratically elected Prime Minister Mohammand Mossadegh in 1953, the hated monarchy was temporarily restored to power. But not for long. And then religious leaders took over control and have continued to control Iran's government ever since. So, we can thank the US government's meddling in another nation's affairs for all of the problems beset on the Iranian people, as well as the rest of the world. We all must work for freedom of thought in every country.

And the need for respect for all must extend these rights to non believers.

No person should be shunted for her or his thoughts and beliefs, as long as their actions are kind, peaceful, and just. No one should be making judgment of others based on his or her personal beliefs.

"Nobody's religion is better than anyone else's religion." Can you say this statement? A whole lot of people cannot. Many people will consider this bad. But if we all look up at the populations of different religions, we should begin to see what I am talking about. And until we all can say and believe this statement, we are never going to achieve world peace. No group of people want any other group of people to tell them what to believe. We all must strive for freedom of thoughts and beliefs. When we respect the freedom of beliefs of others, we are well on the way to world peace.

As we all know, some religions send members of their congregations out into the world to try and convert people to the religion of these missionaries. This makes me uncomfortable. I do not believe that one religion is better than another religion. I believe that everybody should have the freedom to believe or not believe in any religion that they choose. I believe religious leaders should emphasize the importance of respect for the choices of others with their congregants. This can be a great contribution for world peace.

In most religions, there is an intense focus on total servitude to a solitary figure. A god. The congregants are asked again and again to bow their heads in servitude to a single figure. The congregants are asked to pledge their allegiance to this figure and to never question his so called commands. This emphasis on abdicating your freedom of thought must be reconsidered. Authoritarianism is the blind submission to authority. Freedom of thought is precious.

Any threat to an individual's right to freedom of thought should be taken seriously.

Creativity depends on freedom of thought. Crushing a child's or an adult's freedom of thought should be confronted. All problems need solutions. We need freedom of thought to stop the march to wars. We need freedom of thought to conquer Climate Change. The Koch brothers are spending millions of dollars to distort facts so they can continue to sell oil, gas, and chemicals. They are trying to keep you from using your minds to solve serious problems.

I believe that some people need religions to help them feel secure. This does not mean that their religious leaders should pressure them to abandon their rights to freedom of thought. The two are compatible. Religions should help people think for themselves, rather than ask for others to solve their problems.

We all must learn to think better and to think more deeply. Thinking can help us to believe more in ourselves. To have faith in ourselves. Most people need others to encourage them, and show faith in their endeavors. Even religious leaders should be granted freedom of thought. They should be given more freedom by their supervisors to help their congregants gain freedom of thought and gain more self confidence to face a world of great change.

Religions should place far more emphasis on loving thy neighbor.

And this mention of neighbor should not stop at some imagined national border. We must all learn to love people of any color, nationality, or religious belief or non belief. When we accomplish this, wars will be impossible.

We cannot slay those we love.

Animals can be our teachers

As we all know, freedoms are precious. These freedoms were available to animals. Unfortunately, man has overstepped his boundaries, and believed that he has the right to deny freedom to animals. Animals are now kept in cages in zoos and in circuses. This is not fair or right. We must right this wrong.

We need to fund open areas around the world where animals can live in freedom and be safe from poachers who kill them or sell them into captivity. There is no justification for zoos and circuses anymore. We can see all animals in movies and on television. We do not have to keep them in cages for our annual visits. This also extends to fish of all sizes. Fish should have their freedoms as well. It is a disgrace to keep dolphins and porpoises in captivity so you or a trainer can pet them on their noses. The same goes for tiny fish. There is no size that stops for a grant of freedom.

We, citizens of the world, need to develop our sensitivities, so we can feel the desperations of caged and aquariumized creatures. *Animals can be our teachers.* We need to learn to empathize with others' feelings of need. As we refine our sensitivities, we will extend our love , and our world will be a far more pleasant place to inhabit.

Many people who have ample food, still hunt and kill animals. Especially larger animals. Why? Placing a mounted head on the wall of your house does not make you a brave person. It truly identifies you as an insensitive person who stood a long distance from a dumb animal, peered through a very precise gun sight and pulled a trigger.

As populations continue to soar, there is less and less habitat remaining for animals. It is cruel to kill animals for sport. In the very old days, people needed to kill animals to eat. Today, most hunters do not kill animals to eat. They kill because it makes them feel good. I got news for you hunters, you need to find another hobby to make you feel good. Killing dumb animals should not be the choice of good and caring people.

Why not carry a camera instead of a gun and take pictures of beautiful animals trying to survive under very challenging conditions.

You hunters can still enjoy tramping in the woods. You can still enjoy the camaraderie of your pals. Just "stop killing and start loving" the few animals left for us all to admire in the wild. Why not sneak up close to animals and just watch them live?

Many hunters "vacation" at hunting camps where animals are fenced in and are unable to escape being killed by big brave hunters. I believe that these commercial hunting camps should be outlawed. It is bad enough that we are polluting the streams and rivers where wild animals seek water. We should not allow businesses to exist that thrive on the killing of creatures who should have the same right to exist as we do. In 2011, it is time to stop the killing of our fellow creatures.

Two quick examples of lessons still to be learned.

How many of you all felt the terror and needs of the people in Pakistan when 20% of their whole country was flooded in 2010? How many of you felt the fears of the Somali citizens as they fled a historic drought which was ravaging their land and pushing them to flee from their homes in search of water and food in 2011? Need I say more? Think and feel outside of the boxes that we have built around ourselves. If we all begin to expand our caring, we will sense the caring of others towards us, too. This, also, is a building block for world peace.

You may question the above conclusion. But, for a moment put yourself in place of a mother hugging her son or daughter as they are leaving to fight in a war. Empathize with this mother as she wonders each day if she will ever see her child again. If you can do this, you are beginning to sense the importance of all of us venturing into a global spirituality that sanctions peace as a reasonable goal that can be achieved, and must be achieved.

The discovery of DNA has clearly shown that many innocent people have been incarcerated for various crimes that they did not commit.

Executions of man should be banned by the UN, and all international courts. Governments have the capacity to keep dangerous criminals safely away from the public. There is no reason to kill a murderer. We are simply duplicating his/her crime.

What right has any judge to gamble lives, when he/she is aware of our faulty systems of justice? Any person can be a victim of these imperfections.

We must guard against the "lynch mob mentality" of angry people. These people become enraged at a crime and are motivated to seize any person who appears to be guilty. Unfortunately we all don't look innocent. It is quite easy to think you know who is guilty of a crime by simply looking at a person.

And on the other hand, some people are wonderful actors, and can don the face of innocence, when they are quite guilty of crimes.

Capital punishment should be eliminated by all courts in all nations. You can stop this. Speak out. Write letters. Save ourselves from unrestrained lust for revenge. Killing should never be an option for man.

There are way too many people in prisons around the world.

Many are incarcerated because they have displayed dissent against the political leaders of nations. This is wrong and we all must not tolerate taking the freedoms from people for disagreeing with the actions of our governments. Dissent is healthy and exposes faults in governmental behaviour. We must pay attention to dissent and investigate the causes for dissent.

The US Constitution provides protection for people to assemble and voice dissent. I believe every nation should have a constitution with the same protection for dissent. Today, we are witnessing much dissent against existing governments. Unfortunately, many of these governments are killing dissenters, and committing many others to long prison sentences. This is wrong and we all need to protect our freedoms, and the freedoms of others.

Many non violent people are incarcerated because they take drugs.

This is wrong. Taking drugs is personal abuse. It should not be classified as a crime. The sales of illegal drugs should remain criminalized. Drug dealers spread serious mental diseases to the public. Illegal drugs can kill you. They can take away your judgment and place you and your family members in danger. People become mentally sick by taking illegal drugs.

Illegal drugs are addictive. People then cannot tolerate being denied drug usage. The whole drug business is dangerous to all citizens. But I do not think drug users, who are not selling drugs should be placed in prisons. They need hospitalization. They need treatments so they can become free of these drugs. They certainly need psychological therapy to help them be able to cope with their problems without resorting to taking illegal drugs. In the long run, it will be cheaper and safer for all concerned to treat drug users with medical treatment, rather than committing them to incarceration.

Former US President Jimmy Carter stated to Congress in 1977, " The country should decriminalize the possession of less than an ounce of marijuana , with a full program of treatment for addicts. Penalties against possession of a drug should not be more damaging to an individual than the use of the drug itself."

75% of new admissions to state prisons are for non-violent crimes. In 2010, the state of California spent 11% of its budget on prisons and only 7.5% on education! The solution is simple. Stop locking up individual users of illegal drugs. Concentrate enforcement of laws on drug dealers, and fund medical treatment of users. Laws should not be used to deny human rights of freedom. Laws should only be enforced on criminal acts that hurt others, such as drug dealing.

The subject of human rights and animal rights is complex, and yet, simple.

If we expand our sensitivities, the answers will come automatically. As we see abuse, we will react in defense of the abused. The strong should protect the weak and disabled, not bully and harm them. Too many times have we all read of innocent people being attacked and beaten badly, inflicting very serious injuries. Where did all of this anger and insensitivity come from? We need to find the sources that encourage especially young groups of people to harm others.

I recently read of a child having her bike taken from her and then smashed against her body by a group of so called "toughs". Gee, you really have to be tough to beat a little girl with her bike. What a hero! This behaviour evidently gives certain people some sort of twisted enjoyment. We must embarrass the perpetrators who display such cowardice toward the young and weak. What courage can be felt by beating a young child with her bike? This child is now afraid to walk out of her house! Her human rights have been discarded by a bunch of cowardly, stupid young men.

Hey , tough guy, have a go with me. I have only one leg, one eye, and I will be 95 next week!

Bullying must be countered with well thought out public campaigns that illustrate the cowardly behaviour of gangs, mobs, and groups beating up weak people. This a job for all of us, not just schools or churches. The violence of others affects the freedoms of all of us. We need to have the confidence that if we walk out our front door, no gang of cowards will harm us.

For many years, I pursued my hobby of coaching high school basketball. As my wife and I moved around the country, I found myself coaching either a boys' or a girls' basketball team. The one thing I emphasized was sportsmanship. I have never believed in dirty players. I do not believe you should ever try to hurt another player. Unfortunately, my team members experienced this type behaviour which was being taught by some of the other coaches. Cheating and hurting other players are disgraceful choices. Coaches should be fired for teaching this crap. My teams beat the cheaters regardless of their unsavory behaviour. But, we all must be on alert that our children are not being taught the wrong lessons of life.

Today, TV has glamorized the jumping on a fallen opponent and smashing them again and again while they lay on the floor of the X fighting enclosure.

This goes against the teaching I received that stated, " Never hit a man when he is down." And certainly don't kick him! How many times do we all read about gangs of thugs kicking victims while they are on the ground. We can certainly blame the TV shows of exposing our children to X kicking people, and hitting people on the ground. Sportsmanship needs to be taught to our children, so they do not harm others. Dirty fighting results in permanent injuries to others.

 Restraint of anger should be a top subject to be learned by all of us. We must learn that we have no right to " lose our temper" and hurt others. This should be stressed by all parents in all nations.

Another display of cowardice is being displayed by the US government, as they overreact from an irrational fear of terrorism.

They are now resorting to torture of suspected terrorists. And I said suspected, not convicted. These people are not receiving trials to determine if they are guilty of crimes. They actually are being kidnapped, and shipped to secret prisons around the world where they are subjected to torture. These criminal acts by the US government are called renditions. The Human Rights Watch organization has reported that the US government is guilty of over 350 cases of torture of detainees!

No senior level official has ever been charged with these outright criminal acts by a government that keeps claiming that they are a democracy. I do not think a democracy captures people, gives them no legal trial, ships them to hidden prisons, and then subjects them to torture. As an American citizen, I am deeply concerned that this criminal behaviour by my government is still going on. This is the height of denial of human rights.

In 2010, a US law professor named Francis A. Boyle of the University of Illinois College of Law filed a complaint with the International Criminal Court against George W. Bush, Dick Cheney, Donald H. Rumsfeld, George Tenet, Condoleezza Rice, and Alberto Gonzales for their involvement in the practice of renditions (kidnapping people, transporting them to foreign prisons, and making them victims of torture there.).
Professor Boyle also informed the ICC that the Obama Administration publicly stated that it was continuing these criminal acts against people. These are violations of the ICC Crimes Against Humanity under the ICC Rome

Statute. This is certainly one of the more awful things that inspired the title of this book, "Don't Do It Like We Did- in Washington."

The US government is under obligation, under both US law and the Convention against Torture and other Cruel, Inhuman or Degrading Treatment or Punishment, to which the US is a party, to prevent, investigate and prosecute torture and other ill-treatment. Since the US government continues to ignore their own law and international law, we the citizens of the USA need to demand these laws be enforced, and that no more renditions and torture occur.

Torture is a misguided means to obtain information. The problem is that when you are being tortured, you eventually will say anything to stop the pain and anguish. Tortured information is useless.

Citizens cannot abdicate their responsibility, and wait for some small organization to try and right such a terrible wrong.

Lawless behavior by anybody's government must not be tolerated. The human rights of all individuals must be respected. Not just a few, but all. Remember, any person can be accused of being a terrorist. Once accused, an innocent person can be subject to a rendition and torture. It can happen to a friend or relative. It can happen to you. It has been happening for too long and must be stopped.

Obama said he would close Guantanamo prison where many tortures took place when he campaigned for President.

He not only did not close this prison, but under his realm, at least one more secret prison has been built and stuffed with people who have never had legal trials! He has broken this promise, along with a long list of others. We can no longer trust Obama to protect our human rights or our democracy. A democracy cannot exist while tolerating the torture of people. They just don't belong together.

Slavery still exists in the world and yes, in America.

The US State Department statistics reveal that as many as 100,000 people in the USA are enslaved along with an estimated 27 million in other nations! Some of these people are working as domestics in homes where they are denied all freedoms and paid no wages. These numbers include young children sold or kidnapped into slavery and forced to work in brothels.

Some governments, including New Zealand have legalized brothels, claiming that there will be better health conditions for the prostitutes and their clients. I challenge this claim. The New Zealand law does not require blood tests for the prostitutes or their clients. So how does anybody know who is healthy - or not?

Brothels are businesses who attempt to make as much profit as is possible. Prostitutes make more money by having sex with more people. Does each client come into the brothel with a copy of a blood test taken the day of the visit, and the results of that test included. Of course not. Blood testing labs take time to deliver the results of tests. Meanwhile the client may be having sex with people afflicted with AIDs. And the NZ law does not require any type of test, anyway.

Without these impossible safeguards, the client may enter the brothel carrying the AIDs germs and deposit them for all future clients to enjoy. Does the brothel have the prostitute tested after each sexual act? No indeed. The New Zealand lawmakers and public officials base their hope for safety solely, on requiring the use of condoms.

Many babies have been born after the parents depended on birth control by using condoms? Condoms are a first defense against pregnancy and disease, but only the naïve believe they are perfect All it takes to ignore the condom rule, is for a client to offer more money than the ongoing fee. Since the prostitute is willing to sell her body, why should we expect her to refuse a bribe. The New Zealand law is not the answer to having safe sex. If you visit a brothel, you are gambling, and the dice are loaded.

Prostitution is dangerous for the clients. And it is terrible for the prostitutes.

These sexual workers are exposed to real threats of violence by the pimps who are employing them. Many of these prostitutes are young girls who have been forced to work as prostitutes. They are, indeed, enslaved and tortured. They need to be rescued and given the human rights of freedom.

I, personally, attended a university lecture on New Zealand's de-criminalizing prostitution. It appears that New Zealand began dismantling their social welfare programs in the 1980s and also began weakening their regulations on various subjects at that time.

The lecturer stated that studies indicated that one of the major reasons for women to resort to prostitution was economic. As we all know, women are not paid the same wages for the same work done by men. And we also know that women do not share as many management positions as men. This unequal treatment of women is, indeed, causing some women, in desperation, to turn to prostitution.

We, citizens, must not stand by and do nothing for women who need employment. There must be programs started to help women who have been abandoned and women who have been abused. We need funding to be directed towards programs that will give women the opportunity to keep their self esteem and not resort to prostitution. This is all of our responsibilities. Single parent women with children are especially hard hit economically. We need to start programs that will help them and their children. New Zealand is going the wrong way. They need to help the needy and restore their social programs of the 80s.

I also asked the lecturer if there had been a study on the incidence of suicide among prostitutes. She was not familiar with any such study. Prostitution has been around a long time, but so have wars and other nasty things. That does not mean that they have to stay around.

Women who resort to prostitution expose themselves to humiliation, embarrassment, danger, and severe loss of self esteem. Most people hope they can find companions, get married, and raise a family. The odds are against this, for women who resort to prostitution to finding a caring husband, and being able to have children, and raise them in a proper environment. These are all elements that can produce depression and attempts at suicide. We must protect women from entering this sorry sort of employment.

And a quick word on deregulation that the Republicans are always demanding for their clients in finance, manufacturing, and construction.

Several years ago, tiny New Zealand copied the big cats and also cut their regulations, especially in construction. In only 10 years of deregulation, over 80,000 homes were built in New Zealand that leak badly! The estimates of damage range from $ 11 billion to $22 billion! So, we must all remember that every regulation was created because somebody was cheating consumers. Deregulation guarantees that the cheating will come back to haunt us.

This ongoing degradation of females should not ever be legalized and tolerated by a society who claims they care for others.

If you care, you do not allow women to need to sell themselves because they cannot support themselves because of lower wages paid to females. The glass ceiling against promotion of females in many work places, and in many nations must be smashed forever.

If certain nations forbid women to work, they are guilty of slavery. No human should be prohibited the right of freedom to be employed in the work place. By the toleration of this prohibition, they are sentencing females to enslavement and abuse by males.

We, the citizens of the world can stop this by simply demanding our governments boycott the exports of products from these nations. Money talks. No nation can exist without selling to others. How long do you think females would be abused in an oil producing nation, if every government boycotted the purchases of their oil? Isn't this another strong argument to switch from oil? Oil not only is causing Climate Change, but it is corrupting governments to ignore the slavery of women in some of these oil producing nations, such as Saudi Arabia and Kuwait. The sooner we all start driving electric cars the better.

You are never too young to qualify for human rights.

The most widely ratified human rights treaty in the history of the UN is the UN Convention on the rights of the Child. 191 nations signed this treaty. Some of this treaty read "....be protected from economic exploitation and performing any work that that is likely to be hazardous or to interfere with the child's education, or to be harmful to the child's health, or physical, mental, spiritual, or moral or social development." These are beautiful words, but some nations do not enforce any part of this noble law.

One third of the children in sub-Saharan Africa are working long and hard hours. Poverty is certainly one cause. And the future of these children can be brighter if we all work to have a livable minimum wage legislated around the world. The children in poor nations would be the first benefactors. It is time to stop sentencing these youngsters to desperate lifetimes. There are over 200 million children working at hard labor jobs. 70% are employed in agriculture. Over 70 million child workers are under the age of 10. Almost all child workers are denied basic working rights and wages of adult workers. Needless to say, these children are not going to school, and are being condemned to lifetimes of poverty and hard labor.

When the expected propaganda begins against a worldwide livable wage, don't forget these innocent children, whose families are victims of corporate lust for low wages.

And don't forget to empathize with the downtrodden corporate CEOs who need their private jet planes, so they can explore the far reaching golf courses in the world.

And that thought brings up the subject of today's tourism. Many vacationers are totally shielded from the sights of poverty around the world. More and more vacations take place in walled off resorts, that serve as blinders to the eyes and minds of travelers. They visit a country, but do not socialize with the people who live there. I strongly recommend that we all make efforts in our travels to see the local people, talk with them, and sit down and learn something from them.

There are many threats to human rights. Another is the growth of private armies of mercenaries.

The UN is trying to set requirements on these. But, unfortunately, only 32 nations ratified the International Convention against the Recruitment, Use, Financing and Training of Mercenaries in 2001, Few of the larger nations were among the 32 who ratified this much needed legislation.

Armies of mercenaries are a real threat to all of our human rights. They lack the control of a government, and can be directed towards violence against any person or group of persons by the whim of their employer. An example of this threat is the 4 plus years in delay by US courts to act on the alleged killings of 17 civilians and injuring of 20 other civilians in Iraq by armed Blackwater Corporation contractors. These contractors are alleged to have repeatedly fired into a crowd of people, resulting in the above tragedies.

We, the citizens, should be assured by our governments that when we walk outside, the only people we see carrying weapons will be police or members of our nations' armed forces. No more armed civilians with itchy trigger fingers!

A reminder to readers from all nations. It is imperative to work to get governments that truly grant you freedoms.

This requires a sharp separation of government from religious groups, from military, and from corporations. Only with these separations can you be sure of retaining your freedoms. Your government must represent your interests and provide for your welfare. Taxation should be fair and tax payments required from all citizens and corporations. No exemptions or loopholes to the rich or to corporations. We must all share in the funding for the public programs, such as providing education for our children, safety , healthcare, building of infrastructure, and maintenance of all public institutions and infrastructure.

Every person must be able to gain employment in every nation.

These are not the conditions for working people- today in the USA, or in other nations. The minorities in big cities, and young workers, especially, the unemployment rates range from 25% to 50%! There should be no barriers based on gender, race, religion, sexual identity, etc. We all need to work to live. Because different prejudices do exist, it is important to have governmental agencies that a person can contact when they are denied employment because of bias by a potential employer. The playing field must be made level for all people. Nobody should be shunted for being different. Diversity is to be respected and learned from, rather than to be feared and denied employment. Laws must be passed to protect us all, and strictly enforced.

" My skin is white and that makes me smarter, more honest, and a harder worker than you. And if you don't believe me, ask my Daddy."

Racism is still active in many so called democracies. The USA is not innocent of such cruel behavior. Denial of employment of an individual affects a whole family. It is, indeed, cruel. The bigoted employer is guilty of causing great harm to others. The laws must be enforced to erase this mean spirited behaviour. The percentage of unemployment of African Americans is much, much too high, compared to whites, in the USA. Recent studies have confirmed that non-whites in the USA are still being deprived of employment because of their skin color!

There is still plenty of work to be done to right these wrongs towards people of a different color of skin. We can all help fix this terrible problem. If you observe unfair treatment of a person of color, report it to management. Report it to a governmental agency. Don't close your eyes to evil. Fix it. Your silence provides encouragement to wrongful acts. There are methods to report wrongs, and still protect your identity. Be clever, and help others.

Laws, Laws, and more Laws; but no jobs to feed my family!

In 1941, the Fair Employment Practice Committee was created in the USA. In 1964, the Civil Rights Act was passed. This created the Equal Employment Opportunity Commission. In 1965 the Voting Rights Act was passed in the USA. In 1972, the Equal Employment Opportunity Act was passed.

Passing of laws is only the first step to fair behaviour. It must be followed by citizens' reporting violations of these laws. And this must be followed by enforcement of these laws. And the agencies must be funded so they can investigate and enforce laws.

Recently in the USA there is a movement by Republicans to cut funding for many federal agencies, including environmental protection, which affects the health of all people. The newly elected Republicans have also made strong efforts to weaken unions. These unions have been a very effective source of employment for members of minority races, religions, gender, etc. These actions by Republicans are threatening millions of peoples' lives. Americans are under attack by fellow Americans. This is a sad state of affairs. There will be more on this story in another chapter in this book. But, you can put this in the bank, now, Republicans do not care for you. They are bought and paid for by big corporations. PERIOD. White prejudiced workers and small businessmen with small brains who vote Republican, are voting against their own jobs and their own businesses. Don't blame anyone else but yourselves, when you can't find jobs, and your businesses fail. Thank your Republican "friends."

The USA has developed many bad habits in their governing of 308 million people.

One of the most worrisome is the treatment of corporations by bribed elected officials and the rulings of a corporation friendly Supreme Court. The Supreme Court of the USA issues final judgments on selected lawsuits that have been appealed through different levels of the US court system.

In the last few years, the Supreme Courts' rulings have been much too favorable to corporations. A group of international human rights organizations have filed a law suit appealing to the US Supreme Court to overrule judgments that are protecting corporations from being punished for egregious conduct against individuals. This is a serious problem that if not corrected, will allow corporations to continue to escape laws that protect human rights. And we are not talking about minor infractions. The lawsuit addresses killings, arrests, and detentions by corporations!

So, once more I must repeat the warning that allowing corporations to get control of your governments by bribery and other illegal means can be the death of any form of democracy, and your freedoms.

Corporations must be held responsible for their wrongs, and their executives must be held responsible for actions that affect the health and welfare of the public. Corporations and their lobbyists must not be allowed to bribe or otherwise reward legislators. They must not be allowed to infringe on the workings of your government.

I suspect that some of you readers are tiring of my suggestions to get involved and take an active interest in the workings of your governments. This is natural. However, inaction by you and your neighbors has provided your elected officials with blank checks to spend your tax dollars as they choose. The silence of so many has produced an environment of collusion between your so called representatives and check carrying lobbyists from corporations.

These bribes have directed votes to be cast in favor of tax breaks for corporations. *And tax increases for you!* This is only one example of how lack of attention by the many, has enriched a few. "When the cat is away, the mice play." In these situations, we might want to substitute "rats" for "mice". I don't know about you, but if my elected representative is taking bribes, and is voting against my interest, he is not a cute little mouse, he is a rat!

Keep reading if you want to take away the cheese.

EDUCATION

"Education empowers a person for a lifetime.
The more you learn- the more you earn.
Education opens minds to wonders.
Education creates equality for all." ....*H. Greenebaum*

Please don't do what we did all over America! The Organization for Economic Cooperation and Development (OECD) disclosed these statistics: American 15 year olds rank 17th in the world in science, and 25th in math! We now rank 12th among developed nations in college graduations.

America *had* a great public school system.

And then came along former US President George W. Bush. His administration pushed through the phony named "No Child Left Behind" program, that did the opposite as its name. This conglomerate of for profit testing corporations and budget slashing politicians has decimated one of the finest public school systems in the world. They have converted a pleasant learning environment into a scene of fear, stress, and failure. Teachers have been forced to teach for tests instead of teaching for students' joy of learning adventures.

Teachers have been fired en masse around America, as the Republicans attack public programs and march toward their corporate friends' agenda of privatization of all public programs.

The zeal of Republicans' rush to please their benefactors, rich corporations, is historic in its ruthlessness and insensitivity. Teachers and students are the victims of a mad rush for the glint of gold.

The Republicans gain campaign cash to solidify their control of government.

And the corporations get closer to their two goals of privatization of public schools:

#1 They will make lots and lots of money by charging children to attend private –for profit schools.

#2 They can gain control of the curriculum of all schools, so they can distort scientific facts on Climate Change, distort history, distort any information that could possibly affect their profit lines.

Yes, this is happening in America -today!

The Republicans have captured the majority of state legislatures and governorships. They are cutting severely the budgets for public schools. Teachers are being fired en masse. Classroom sizes have increased from the 20s to the high 30s, and high 40s with no ends in sight. Schools who fail the national tests are being closed, rather than fixed. With the budget cuts, the failures are sure to accelerate. A teacher who has her/his class size doubled is in a lose-lose situation.

The phony propaganda of " bad teachers" is deluding the public from the real cause of school failures. No public program can succeed without proper funding. The Republicans know this, but they are faithfully marching to the tune of corporate privatization. The very core of democracy in America is crumbling before our very eyes. This is the result of allowing corporations to run amuck. This is the sad lesson for other nations to absorb and prevent from happening to their citizens.

Nations that blend social welfare and economic balance are producing the best schools in the world for their children.

Examples of these successes are in Denmark, Sweden, Norway, and Finland. These nations not only have funded and fondled their public schools, but they also have provided their citizens with wonderful national healthcare programs.

Corporations hate social programs because they will be liable for taxes to fund them. And the Republicans' friend, Barack Obama, does *not* defend them!

In contrast, over 51 million Americans have no health insurance. Another 50 million or more Americans have health insurance with such high deductibles that they cannot afford to go to hospitals! America has a President, Obama, who has refused to consider a government run healthcare program for all citizens. He has steadfastly defended the profits of the health insurance companies. His coziness with corporations is costing thousands of lives of Americans, who die each year because of the lack of medical care.

America's public school system is under attack by <u>more </u>than just corporations.

It is being manipulated by one very rich billionaire, Bill Gates. Mr. Gates is the richest man in the USA. He is extremely interested in the US public school system and has spent hundreds of millions of dollars to make changes in it. But there is some curious information about Mr. Gates you should know. He does not have a Doctorate in education. He does not have a Masters degree in education. In fact, he does not even have a graduation diploma from a college. He has a meager two and one half years of college! He is a college drop out! I ask you, do you think a man who has no advanced educational knowledge should be telling schools all over the country how to educate your children? Well, that is what is happening on a grand scale, today, in the USA.

Here is a condensed summary of Bill Gates and his foundation's meddling in our public school systems. Gates is financing educators to pose alternatives to the established policies. His foundation is paying many analysts who interpret education issues for the media. He is giving money to media organizations. In 2009, his foundation spent $ 78 million on advocacy of his ideas for the US schools. Many of the so called experts on education that you see on TV are paid by the Gates foundation. Gates' foundation's 2009 tax filing contains 263 pages, of which there are 360 education grants.

Gates is an important financier of charter schools, which have been the subject of much controversy.

Charter schools have less regulations than public schools , and are free to pick and choose students for their schools. Charter schools' selectivity of students allows them to escape the low test scores of disadvantaged students, that public schools are required to accept. They also escape the costs of assistance to these needy students.

Mr. Gates' billions allows him to spend as much money as he chooses to influence school policies. His money certainly allows him to fund research on educational issues, and he has the choice on how to use the results of his funded research.

He has donated millions of dollars to the National Governors Association and the Council of Chief State School Officers, *which developed the national standards,* and to Achieve, a non-profit organization that *coordinates the writing of these standardized tests.*

National standardized tests have been a disaster for children's education in America!

Today, these tests dominate public school education. They are the greatest obstacle to good teaching. Teachers are now forced to teach for tests. The students are denied the joy of learning because so much time is required to instruct for the tests. Teachers have had their talents and skills dulled by the constant pressure of the national tests. Students are the victims of this flawed program of testing.

Bad decisions are forced upon the public school system by the results of the tests. Good schools are being closed. Good teachers are being fired. Good administrators are being fired. The results of these tests are frequently misinterpreted by the requirements of the very faulty national testing law. The results of the tests do not contribute toward the education of the students.

I suspect this national testing law was not written to improve public education, but was aimed at destroying public education!

Parents of public school students need to meet with teachers and learn how awful this testing program is for their children. Parents need to demand that the testing law be repealed, so their children can be relieved of this bad program. If parent s do not respond, most of the good teachers will be gone, and the children will be dumbed down by this great loss of fine educators.

In 2010, Gates' foundation donated $ 500,000. to the Foundation for Educational Excellence ,which was founded by Jeb Bush, the brother of George W. Bush.

The lesson to be learned from this information is that nobody should be allowed to accumulate billions of dollars. Because the power that goes with these huge globs of money can and will assert far more power than is healthy for any real democracy.

Public schools should be run by the government for the public.

No rich man or group of rich men should be allowed to influence the education of our children. They have not been elected to pursue this role. They may have all the best intentions, but this does not matter. No person is perfect. No person has all the answers. Children's education must not be kidnapped and manipulated by the rich.

Here are some examples of how corporations have already been interfering and intruding on our children's schooling:

After the Exxon Valdez oil spill in Alaska, Exxon wrote a lesson plan emphasizing the wildlife flourishing in their habitat, *in contrast* to the numerous deaths of these creatures from Exxon's spilled oil.

Oil company, BP, helped write *an environmental* curriculum for 6 million students in California.! This is the same company which was involved in the giant oil spill in the Gulf of Mexico!

Scholastic, the *largest publisher* of children's textbooks, published a 4th grade curriculum entitled, "The United States of Energy", which emphasized the "clean" image of dirty coal. This curriculum was produced in collaboration with the American Coal Foundation!

Scholastic's Parent & Child magazine collaborated with the SunnyD juice company to promote their juice products, and awarded 20 books to each class which sent in 20 SunnyD labels. Consumer organizations have been very critical of SunnyD juice because it has *such high sugar* and *very low fruit juice*. Some of these organizations call SunnyD juice – "junk juice."

Scholastic has also collaborated with *Shell Oil Company to write science curriculum!*

Scholastic published a teacher's guide entitled, " Shedding Light on Energy" which was on Scholastic's web site along with the *Shell Oil curriculum*. The teacher's guide was a collaborated product between Scholastic and the *US Chamber of Commerce*. The <u>Chamber has consistently denied that there is Climate Change</u>! And we can easily guess who are some of the members of this profit polluted business group.

Scholastic has collaborated with several other corporations, including *McDonald's* restaurants.

Finally, the public acted!

In May 2011, several environmental organizations and teacher groups in the USA combined to *blast these intrusions on children's education by corporations*. Scholastic made several positive changes because of the outcries from the public. This happened because the public was educated, got organized, and got tough. This is the formula for change that can bring change in all of our countries. Learn – Mobilize – Demand!

Education is one of the most important tools to help people escape poverty.

We must protect public education so all children have the opportunity to learn. We must help poor nations build schools for their children. And we must make sure that the curriculum in all schools is pure.

Education must be separated from corporations and from religions.

Children must be protected, so they can learn the truths. They must also be protected so they maintain freedom of thoughts. Freedom of thought is essential for them to be creative and be able to question subject matter. We learn best when our minds are not suppressed by others. Freedom of thought is precious for our treasures – our children.

Education only succeeds when there is a partnership of government, educators, and parents.

It will not work if your government passes bad laws impacting education. It will not work if your government is controlled by corporations who are trying to sabotage public programs, so they can make profits by privatizing them. It will not work if governments continue to cut the funding of educational institutions.

It will not work if parents shirk their responsibilities to participate in their children's education.

It will not work if parents are " too busy" to attend school activities. It will not work if parents are " too busy" to attend parent/teacher conferences. It will not work if parents do not monitor what is happening to their children's education by the mistakes I have listed above. And it will not work if parents do not encourage their children to excel in their studies.

Parents who complain about their children getting too much homework, are sabotaging their children's futures. Hard work never hurt anyone. Parents' cooperation and participation in their children's education is a must. Parents must inspire their children to learn. The love of reading by parents can be a golden model for children to copy. Watching TV must be rationed, and monitored continuously. TV violence must be avoided. Raising children is not a leisure pursuit. The most important demonstration of love is communication. Parents must learn the art of gentle communication with their beloved children. There is much too much abuse of children. There should be no abuse. Many parents need to learn anger management. Drinking alcohol and taking drugs can easily result in child abuse.

Education is a subject not limited to children. Parents must take their roles as fathers and mothers seriously . They should try and learn as much as they can about being the best parents that they can. Books can help. Conference with teachers can help. Seeking help from psychological therapists can be a big help.

I will close this chapter by saying that I wish all parents the best of luck. I now have children in their fifties, and I still consider myself a father. I, of course, can only offer some advice at this point in their lives, but I and you will always be parents, and I hope love will flow between you and your children forever.

BAD HEALTH = AMERICAN DIET + LACK OF HEALTHCARE

"Patents on pills guarantees kills.
Want to be a doctor to make money? Go to a business school!
Eat meat and die young." …. H. Greenebaum

Good health should be apparent in the world's largest economy.

I said," Should Be."Americans are one of the fattest populations in the world. And one of the sickest, too.

Each chart on the incidence of diabetes indicates the growth of diabetes II increases with the percentage of overweight people. America wins hands down. We get the blue ribbon for eating more and dying more. So when you see a framed picture of a blue ribbon steer in a restaurant- run, don't walk back outside. Americans' appetite for beef and pork is only as great as their appetite for cheese, butter, eggs, and milk. The problem with this diet is it is killing lots of people.

Meat and dairy contain huge quantities of saturated fat.

Saturated fat clogs arteries. When your arteries get clogged, you have heart attacks and strokes because the blood cannot get in and out of your heart. It is that simple. It has been that simple for a long time. But, as this book continues to emphasize, corruption can distort logic. And now you will see how corruption has managed to kill lots of Americans by withholding information that could have saved their lives.
There are two books that should be read by everybody who eats food.

One is called, " The China Study." It is the most comprehensive study of nutrition ever conducted. The co-authors are Dr. T. Colin Campbell and his son, Thomas M. Campbell II. This study was conducted by the top food scientists in the world from 3 countries, Oxford University of Great Britain, Cornell University of the USA, and from China. These scientists chose a populous area in China where the citizens are very little afflicted with heart disease or cancer. They did all types of research and concluded that their particular diet was the cause of their good health.

One of the most important findings was that the Chinese diet *starved* the growth of cancer in contrast to the findings that revealed that the consumption of meats and dairy *fueled* the growth of cancer!

Collusion between government and food companies is dangerous for your health

The US government issues a chart each year claiming that eating certain kinds of food is the key to good health . The people on the commission that compose this chart are not scientists. They all are lobbyists from the meat and dairy industries! Small wonder that we all believe that we need to eat meat to gain proteins. That is an outright lie!

 Almost every food contains proteins. The key to eating healthy proteins is to avoid any type meat or dairy product. A diet of grains, vegetables and fruits is the best diet to stay healthy. This diet is called the Vegan diet. Some of the greatest athletes in the world are Vegans! The strongest animals in the world are Vegans- elephants and horses. The tallest animal in the world is a Vegan – giraffes. The answer to good health and strength has been in front of our eyes all these years, munching on leaves, grass, and grains.

The second book that every eater should read is called, " Prevent and Reverse Heart Disease."

The author is Dr. Caldwell B. Esselstyne, Jr. The Foreword of this book was written by Dr. T. Colin Campbell, author of The China Study. Dr. Esselstyne is one of the most prominent cardiologists in the world. He worked at the Cleveland Clinic which is renowned for its knowledge and treatments of heart disease.

Dr. Esselstyne did a great deal of research on heart disease and concluded that the Vegan diet is the safest diet. His book tells stories of when other cardiologists have referred their seriously ill patients to him, and his great success in saving their lives by switching them to the Vegan diet. Dr. Esselstyne also recognized that switching to a Vegan diet was not that easy. So, his wife helped his patients and readers of his book, by inserting 150 pages of recipes in his book. These well thought out and delicious meals make the transition from an unhealthy diet to a life saving diet easy.

Both of these books can be bought from Amazon.com for $10. each. I have no financial relationship to Amazon.com or to the two book authors. I just want you to know where you can buy these books, and that they are affordable.

I do have a personal story to tell about my diet though.

On April 30, 2005, I awoke with a tightness in my chest. I also was sweating. The tightness did not hurt, but it was in no hurry to leave either. I suggested to my wife that I should go to a doctor. She stated, "We are driving to a hospital right now." Fortunately, I listen to my wife a lot. It has been the secret to our 25 years of happy marriage. When we arrived at the hospital, I was whisked into a special heart section and tests were immediately begun. I stayed at the hospital while the tests continued.

At first, the tests did not indicate a heart attack. Fortunately, I had excellent doctors who continued the tests and they finally found some small indications that something was wrong inside. I was very scared when this news was given to me. My three children rushed to the hospital to be by my side. When the surgeon took a look inside my arteries, he discovered that I had not one, but two major arteries clogged! He inserted two stents into each artery. (A stent is a tiny spring like cylinder that expands the artery so blood can flow freely back and forth from the heart.) This operation was performed on May 2, 2005.

After the operation, the doctor prescribed a statin drug called Lipitor. Within hours of swallowing the Lipitor medicine, I felt extreme pains in several muscles in my body. My doctor was called in and he changed the prescription to one half of the usual strength. Again, I was besieged with lots of pains in my muscles. The doctor then was called and I announced to him that I was not going to take any more of these pills, but I was going to "eat my medicines." The doctor had a puzzled look on his face, and asked me " what do you mean?" I answered, " I am not going to die from taking medicines. I am going to avoid whatever was responsible for clogging my arteries, and only eat healthy foods that do not clog my arteries." I announced this decision on May 3, 2005 while I was still recovering from the installation of 4 stents into my arteries.

The side effects that I had encountered were a symptom of a life threatening condition called Rhabdomyolysis. If I had continued to suffer from this condition, my kidneys could have failed, causing me to die. My instincts saved my life.

It is now 2011. I have not taken any medicines for over 6 years! I work out strenuously in a health club 3 times a week. My wife and I hike up steep mountains. Before moving to New Zealand we hiked up mountains in Colorado, where the beautiful Rocky Mountains loom up over 14,000 feet into the sky. We biked miles and miles up and down hills in Colorado. I lift weights at a pace that provides both strength and stamina. I ride on stationary bikes and utilize the elliptical exercise machines for stamina. I do not baby myself. I doubt it there are many 82 year old men that can do what I do in one hour of constant exercise and weight lifting.

I totally endorse the Vegan diet for saving my life and allowing me to lead a robust lifestyle. Oh, and I almost forgot, I walk our Siberian Husky dog every day for 35 to 50 minutes, too. Her name is Kenzie and she has red and white fur and the weirdest blue eyes. My wife and most pedestrians think she is very cute. I am not sure of that, but she can jump real high and lands on our bed every morning with a big bang! When she lies down, she crosses her front legs, and stretches her back legs like a frog. She is a hoot!

I would like to ask the American media why they have not publicized the outstanding results of the China Study.

This study was done years ago. Doctors Campbell and Esselstyne have tried to get this message out for a long time. They are now up in age. They need to see this news shouted out by the media! I suspect that a few industries have something to do with this huge cover up of life saving information. Let's see. Who would NOT like to see these two books read? Hmmm. Cattle growers. Hog growers. Meat companies. Dairy farms. Ice cream manufacturers. Ham sandwich makers. (I used to eat ham sandwiches every day of my life.) I also loved to eat roast beef and steaks. I adored ice cream. But, the motivation of staying alive is stronger than my disappointed taste buds.

The Vegan diet is a lifetime change.

No cheating. Well, maybe a tiny bit. (But I mean tiny.) Oh, back to the list of guys who would hate you to read these two books. Everyone in the meat industry. Yes, this includes sea food, too. I was raised on Chesapeake Bay crabs. I loved shrimp. Nevermore. Nevermore. (Sounds like the raven from Edgar Alan Poe's book.) The exclusion of milk, eggs, bacon, cheese, etc. is a must. You will be surprised to learn that saturated fat is in all of the oils that other people use to cook with. All of the oils! I know, some of you have read somewhere that some kinds of oils are healthy. Ain't so. Read about the oils in Dr. Esselstyne's book. He knows. He has treated enough patients who have heart disease to know a whole lot.

Another important study that has been ignored by our darling US media

About 4 years ago I came across a flyer written by the Physicians Committee for Responsible Medicine. This organization of doctors has an office in Washington, DC Their web site is www.PCRM.ORG They publicized a study that showed that people with Diabetes II who switched to a Vegan diet and stuck with it for 26 days, were amazed that the symptoms of diabetes began to disappear. Many of them were able to stop taking their medicines. Follow ups revealed that those who stuck with the vegan diet had no more symptoms of diabetes.

Once again, why haven't we seen big headlines about these discoveries? This study was performed in 1999. Of course, this would be bad for the advertisers of pills, wouldn't it be? I am afraid that there is an epidemic of corruption in America that is pervasive. There is much work to be done. The information in this book can save people's lives. We all must expose the corruption in our countries and stamp it out. It is much too dangerous to tolerate. We must be provided with truths from our media. I will write more on this in the final chapter in this book.

"How do I switch to a Vegan diet? What do I eat?"

Here is a simple method to buy healthy food. I call it the 3 Ss. Look on the back of every single thing that will eventually go into your mouth. Everything! You will find a small chart listing the saturated fat, sugar, sodium, and other ingredients. Make sure you check the Saturated Fat, Sodium, and Sugar contents. Look for zero or near zero. Compare the different Brands of the same food. Always, select the one with less Saturated Fat, Sugar, and Sodium. It is that simple.

You will find more and more foods with zero content. Be careful. This is more important than buying a car! Your life depends on what you eat. Some countries are less particular about the size of the print type on these charts.

Demand that your government requires this information to have large letters and numbers.

A trick that some food companies use should be stopped. After you look at the quantity, look at the serving size. Different companies vary the size of the serving size. For ex. if one cookie company say only one gram of Sat. fat, but describes the serving size as one cookie, and another cookie company says 2 grams of Sat.fat, but their serving size is 6 cookies. Which cookie is the worse to eat? Study this example. Figure it out.

There are many, many substitutes for meat, cheese, ice cream, etc.

Food manufacturers are now able to produce similar foods that taste good! Visit natural food stores and study their selections. You will be quite surprised.

If there is very little selection in stores near you; then you are looking at an opportunity to become rich. Open a store. Open a restaurant. Sell these products to stores and restaurants. We eat a substitute for ice cream that tastes the same! We drink soy milk which has no saturated fat! We eat soy and rice cheese that tastes the same as cheese derived from milk. There are many substitutes for meat too.

Dine in Indian, Chinese, and Mediterranean restaurants and ask for meatless meals.

Millions of people in these countries do not eat meat. If you go into a Subway restaurant, ask for the veggie patty sandwich. The patty is a substitute for meat and is very tasty and filling. Ask the clerk to put in all kinds of vegetables, and make sure they do not put any salt, pepper, or any sauce or oil. Eat the sandwich and taste the patty and vegetables. You will be surprised that you do not have to drown your food with all kind of sauces and oils.

When you switch to a Vegan diet, you will have more money left in your pocket! Yes, it costs less to be a Vegan. No more expensive meats and seafood. When you eat out and ask for a meal without meat, the price is reduced. You save again. Your grocery bill will be lower. This is a win win situation. Not only do you become healthy and live longer, but you get richer too.

Another excellent reason to stop eating meat is that there are a lot of dangerous stuff now being added to the food that animals are forced to eat.

Because corporations are crowding cattle, hogs, and chickens into small fenced, barred, and walled in areas the animals are getting sick. These unhealthy conditions are causing the animals to die from diseases. So, the corporations are stuffing all kinds of antibiotics into their food. They also are stuffing growth hormones into their food so the animals grow bigger and fatter. They also are stuffing metals, and who knows what else. All of these additives end up in your stomachs.

Research has shown that these additives are bad news for humans who consume these meats. The numbers are frightening. 70 percent of the antibiotics sold in America are in the meat you are eating. This produces antibiotic-resistant bacteria which can kill you. Many consumer and environmental organizations have joined in a law suit against the FDA to force them to stop these procedures. However, time will tell how this will work out. Some law suits travel slowly through the US court system and take years to settle, after appeals, etc. A quick way to avoid consuming these contaminated meats, is to simply stop eating meat from corporate "factory farming." Since it is difficult to find out where meat is coming from, the simplest way to stay healthy is to just plain stop eating meat.

The Center for Science in the Public Interest (CSPI) filed a regulatory petition to urge the US Department of Agriculture (USDA) to stop the distribution of anti-biotic-resistant strains of Salmonella which has been found in ground beef and poultry. CSPI food safety staff attorney Sarah Klein stated, " The only thing worse than getting sick from food is being told that no drugs exist to treat your illness." This is another confirmation that eating meat can kill you. And I do not restrict this to eating in America, because American meat can be exported to your country, or the agricultural technology could already be operating in your country. So make sure your government is protecting you, and not corporations.

Another intrusion on farming around the world is the corporation Monsanto's sales and distribution of GMO (Genetically Modified Organisms).

Once more a corporation has found ways to make more money in a controversial manner. I don't know about you, but I don't want to eat something that has been genetically modified. The Public Patent Foundation and the Cornucopia Institute, which has 4,000 members, mostly organic farmers, are suing Monsanto to prevent the contamination of their farms from GMO seeds. I believe that every government should have much more stringent regulations to protect our food from new fangled ideas that may endanger our health.

Collusion between bribed US government and health insurance companies

America has or perhaps had a very large economy. But, in spite of all this accumulated wealth, many , many Americans die each year due to lack of access to medical care. Over 51 million Americans have no health insurance! One study estimated that 45,000 Americans die each year from a lack of health insurance! As many as 50 more million have such high deductibles on their insurance policies, that they are unable to afford to go to hospitals! The private insurance companies have raised and are continuing to raise their premiums to such heights that they are choking the American economy.

Far too much of an American family's income is sucked away by greedy health insurance companies. These companies are reaping huge profits at the cost of lives, and the economic health of the US economy. The huge monthly bite out of the average family's income is encroaching on their total spending. Families are trying to balance their budgets, but are failing because of health insurance companies' lust for more and more gold from hard working Americans. 62% of personal bankruptcies in the USA are caused by medical expenses!

Every state has a state insurance agency that is supposed to protect the public. But that is not happening. Unfortunately, quite a few of the state legislatures failed to give these state agencies the power to regulate the premiums! Gee, I wonder if any of the insurance companies' lobbyists had anything to do with these peculiar circumstances. Insurance companies are free to charge as much as they choose, and they choose to charge more and more and more.

I, personally, have been selling health insurance for over 12 years. In that short a time, I have witnessed an industry running amuck. When I first started selling health insurance, people selected a $250 deductible and received a policy with an affordable monthly premium. (A deductible must be paid by the patient before the insurance company begins to pay for your medical or hospital expenses.) Today, only 12 years later, people are now choosing deductibles that range up to $25,000! The higher the deductible you choose the lower is your monthly payment. When a person gets sick and the doctor tells them they need to go to a hospital, they used to pack a small suitcase and go to the hospital. Today, the person first finds out what the hospital will cost. When they are told that they must pay their deductible first, many choose to not go to the hospital. And we all know what happens to them after that sad decision.

This deplorable catastrophe is the result of bribes to government officials who were supposed to be voting to protect the citizens.

The insurance companies have also been able to block any type of real national health plan from being enacted.

The obvious solution to this threat to Americans' health was to expand Medicare to all Americans. Medicare is now only available to people over the age of 64, plus to only the very severely disabled of any age. By expanding Medicare to all, every American could be free of the private health insurance companies' intrusions on their income. Medicare is a government run program that has no profits involved. The age 65 and up population enjoys belonging to Medicare and has no complaints from this government run program. The only opposition to expanding Medicare to all citizens comes from the insurance companies.

So how come the federal government has not expanded Medicare to all citizens? If anything ever confirms the depth of corruption in the American government, this is the final verification. There is no possible explanation to the lack of a national healthcare program in America except bribery.

Americans can no longer afford to pay the obscenely high premiums that health insurance companies charge. The government from the US President on down has turned their backs on the citizens of America! Before the so called health reform bill was voted on, President Obama allowed health insurance companies' lobbyists to visit him in his office, where they "convinced" him to oppose Medicare for All Americans. Obama then did not support expanding Medicare for All and valiantly protected the health insurance companies from any type of real competition from a single payer national healthcare program.

When the US Senate held a public hearing, Democratic Senator Max Baucus ordered Security to remove doctors and nurses from the so called public hearing, so these honest advocates for a single payer government run program could not even be heard! Instead of objecting to this Senator's action, President Obama voiced his support for Senator Baucus. This is what is happening in our so called democracy, that Americans used to enjoy.

The health reform bill that was passed by a bribery saturated Congress is a phony bill that has parts of the legislation not even taking effect until the year 2014 ! When Medicare was created, it was operating In less than one year. And this was way back in 1965 when there were no computers!

Today, if Medicare had been expanded to all Americans, it could have been accomplished in weeks. Why? Because by expanding health insurance to all citizens, three giant agencies of well trained federal employees could have been merged into Medicare. The Veterans Administration which covers all military personnel could have merged into Medicare. And the Medicaid agency which covers all the poor could have merged with Medicare.

Instead, we have a 4 year or longer delay in enacting a phony reform bill that gives a fraction of the care that Americans could have gained from Medicare. And, of course, would have cost American families a fraction of what private insurance companies are now stealing out of their pockets.

There is another thing happening as I write about the sad story of American health care.

President Obama has gone back on his campaign promises of protecting Americans' Social Security, Medicaid, and Medicare. He has offered to cut $ 650 billion from these vital safety nets for Americans, in order to get the Republicans to pass the annual Budget! Whatever happens in August 2011 to settle this threat against the American financial standing, you can be assured that the American people are going to be short changed. Lies about these three programs must be answered with facts.

Social Security does not have financial problems. Its only problem is that politicians have been borrowing from its reserve to try and balance the budget for years! Americans have been paying into this program for years. And politicians have been borrowing these funds to pay for everything, from waging wars that many Americans have opposed, to cutting $ 2.5 trillion in taxes for the super rich!

Medicare would never have financial problems if it would be offered to all Americans. Today, Medicare is paying claims for the most vulnerable people, the elderly and the severely disabled. If Medicare covered all Americans, it would have added income from the many healthy younger citizens.

And of course, we must consider that parts of the Medicare program passed by ex-President George W. Bush banned Medicare from negotiating lower prices for medicines! This was passed by a bribed Congress, even though other federal agencies, like the Veterans Administration, have had the rights to negotiate lower prices for years. What was the rationale for preventing negotiating lower prices for medicines? Maybe it had something to do with the presence of corporation paid lobbyists while this new addition to Medicare was being written into law?

And this is another lesson to be learned in advance of reforming the governments around the world. Please don't do it like we did. Too many people are suffering from these misdeeds, already. Never, never let lobbyists near the people writing laws. They pollute the process.

Every country should have a national healthcare program for all of its citizens. This program must be government run, so there is no conflict between profit for the few and care for the many.

In fact, I suggest that there should be public debate on the subject of profit on several vital needs for citizens.

I am referring to the need for medicines as a good example. By now, we certainly understand why patents were placed on medicines. But is that right? Should we restrict the distribution of life saving medicines to the wealthy? Of course not. So let's get rid of patents on medicines. The only argument for this is that pharmaceutical manufacturers will claim that they invested money in the research. But, how true is that?

The US National Institute of Health pays huge sums of money for drug research. Let's skip the spin and get to facts and solutions. I suggest that every government invest in research for medicines and then offer the results to all manufacturers. No more patents on vital finds for the welfare of mankind.

Every human being should be entitled to have access to medicines. Medicines should be a nonprofit situation. The governments can manufacture medicines by contract to the lowest bidders. Our governments should never choose profits over welfare and safety for citizens. This should be the guiding principle in good governorship.

The manufacturing of medicines and the research of medicines is deeply corrupted.

The research of medicines that has been funded by corporations is very suspect. By allowing corporations to fund research, it opens the door to corruption. And it is happening big time! With corporate funding, the corporations control the results of the tests. If the tests reveal life threatening side effects, the corporations can bury the tests, or distort the results of the tests.

Many, many medicines have been approved by the US FDA, (US Food and Drug Administration) and later found to be extremely dangerous! The FDA needs a new administration and much investigation into the financial affairs of every member and every candidate for employment with this agency. No agency is more important than the agency who is approving medicines and food.

It is sad to report that the US FDA is also guilty of rushing through approvals that result in deaths of Americans and citizens of other nations, too.

The US FDA is also guilty of many delays in banning already approved drugs that have been discovered to be killing and harming patients. There have been many instances where Europe has yanked a dangerous drug off the market, and the FDA has waited several YEARS before banning the same drug! The FDA needs more funding and much stricter regulations that protect the public from cheating corporations. No person employed by the FDA should have any financial relationship with any private corporation. PERIOD!

There is another problem with American health care. The doctors!

When I was much younger, doctors used to make house calls. I am sure very few Americans today have experienced a house call. It is actually a visit in your home by a doctor. Believe it or not, folks, doctors used to make lots of house calls every day! And the doctor not only talked to the patient, but he/she talked to the family. You can still see this in the movies. But that is the only place it occurs now, in America. Part of this problem is related to health insurance companies. And part is not.

Health insurance companies not only are uncontrolled in their gouging of premiums, but they have taken some major controls of doctors as well.

In their constant search for more profits, these corporations have invaded the medical practice of doctors. Depending on insurance companies, and the types of insurance policies that patients have, doctors are compelled to follow certain procedures to be eligible for remuneration.

One such requirement is the time spent with patients. Yes, there is a time clock ticking when your doctor appears in the waiting room. Some doctors follow the instructions by the insurance companies very precisely. That is bad. Because a restriction of time discussing the symptoms of an undiagnosed disease can be a threat to your life! There are many, many diseases out there. It takes time to make a correct diagnosis.

It also may require expensive tests to find the diagnosis.

And, once more , the insurance companies have chosen to intrude on the doctors' procedures. Doctors are actually told to avoid expensive testing. As an example, if you have a sore leg, a doctor will usually choose an x-ray which costs $10 versus a MRI which can cost over $ 1,000. Even if this lame leg does not heal, some doctors may continue to avoid prescribing a MRI test. I have met patients who have had to threaten doctors with litigation, etc. to get the proper testing of their ailments.

Today, one must be assertive to get the medical treatment necessary for your health in the USA. Under these conditions, the meek will perish. This was not the way doctors used to practice medicine. American medical care has changed. And not for the better.

Several years ago, my personal doctor died. I found a new doctor who did not rush his diagnosis of my ailments. This doctor was very conscientious. I recommended him to my friends. And then he was fired! The insurance companies stopped paying him because he was costing them too much money. That is what is happening in America today. The doctors that try to be good doctors are under great stress from the insurance companies. Americans' healthcare is at risk.

I, personally, have had some very bad experiences with doctors who follow the procedures of the insurance companies.

I believe there are two types of people practicing medicine today. Those who truly care for people, and those who should have gone to business school, because their focus is only on how much money they can make. And there is a lot of money to be made. The lowest paid doctors are the ones who should be paid the most. They are the doctors who make the primary diagnosis. They are called family doctors. Their salaries average $ 200,000. per year.

There is a shortage of family doctors because specialists get paid far more. Specialists' salaries range from close to $ 300,000. all the way up to almost - $700,000 per year!

There also is another way for doctors to make money.

Pharmaceutical manufacturers send out representatives to visit doctors and supposedly explain the details of newly released medicines. Unfortunately, this is not all that takes place in doctors' offices. Some reps also offer incentives to doctors to prescribe the medicines of their employer. These incentives can include some very expensive fully paid vacations. And they can be outright bribes of money ranging up to $50,000. and more! So, the crooked doctors take the money and over prescribe medicines to unsuspecting patients. And the doctors get rich, and you may die from taking the wrong medicines!

We also have a real problem with US doctors picking and choosing patients.

Many doctors refuse to accept poor patients whose bills are paid by the federal program entitled Medicaid. Why? Because Medicaid pays less money for care for the poor.

When I was a young guy, doctors donated a half day or even a full day every week to care for the poor. They received no money for this noble work. Those days are gone, except for a very, very few wonderful doctors who are left. I met a married couple who both practiced medicine in North Carolina who do care more for the poor than for money. I admire them greatly.

It is very difficult for poor people to find doctors who accept Medicaid patients. Is this the way to treat people with less money? Of course not. But it is the way medicine is practiced in the USA today. America is not a good place to live if you are poor and get sick.

This can be solved.

Each state or province in a nation should have a licensing program for their doctors. This program should prohibit doctors from refusing to serve all the sick. No picking and choosing. If a doctor is found guilty of denying medical care, he/she should have their licenses revoked. That will solve that problem real fast.

Not only are the doctors not willing to care for the poor, but the Republicans and President Obama are targeting the Medicaid programs for deep cuts in funding. So these cuts will make it even more difficult for poor people to find a doctor. Lack of access to medical care is responsible for the deaths of thousands of Americans every year. This is not a small problem in America.

There is a great shortage of doctors in small towns in the USA. Once more money is the consideration that causes the shortage. There obviously are less rich people in small towns than in big cities. So, the doctors follow the money into the larger cities.

There are solutions.

France and Great Britain offer free medical schooling for their students after they graduate high school. America does not. The average American student who graduates from an American medical school leaves with a huge debt of $150,000 or more. If every nation offers free medical schooling, the government should have some authority on supplying the needs for their citizens. Doctors should be made available for all areas, not just the affluent areas. And there should be incentives for doctors to move to rural areas and inner city areas. These incentives could be tax reductions.

Since most nations have national healthcare programs for all of their citizens, the governments can also control their costs better than in the USA where corruption has prevented these cost controls. Every governmental agency should have the authority to negotiate lower prices for all products and services. No more preferential treatment for "your friends."

You are reading about a lot of corruption in the US medical industry. I am not yet finished.

There is a lot of government and corporation money going toward research in the medical field. For a moment, let's consider the manner in which this money and research is monitored. I am not satisfied that corporations should even be considered eligible for this type of venture. How can we trust profit driven corporations to handle negative results from their funded research? There must be a whole lot more supervision than is now available.

As for government funded research, I suspect that some scientists may be tempted to delay conclusions as long as the grant money lasts. What incentives are offered for fast research? What penalties are there for deliberately delaying completing research? Funding must be made available for inspections and investigation of government and corporation funded research. Strict penalties should be legislated for phony research, distorted research, and deliberate delaying of research.

The success of every national healthcare program in every nation depends on funding. We must vote in people who recognize this need and support the proper funding of their national healthcare programs.

And, finally who picks the research targets?

Is it possible that surgeons are replacing hips and knees because no money has been spent researching the regeneration of cartilage in these joints? Most surgery on joints is caused by a condition called " bone on bone". This translates into the wearing away of all of the cartilage. It is possible that cartilage could be regenerated by injections of a person's own stem cells.

Surgeons performing hip and knee replacements are among the highest paid doctors. Are they interested in discoveries of how to provide treatments that would eliminate surgery? I doubt it.

Are these surgeons being consulted by officials about how the government money should be spent on research? I do not know. But we should know more of these particulars. There is an old saying that still is true, " The devil is in the details."We, citizens, must delve into details and kick the devils out. The public should demand transparency of the targeting of our tax dollars toward research.

There are millions of deaf and near deaf people being victimized by obscenely high prices for hearing aids in the USA. I am guessing that the majority of the hearing impaired cannot afford to buy hearing aids in the USA. I see lots of full page ads in large city newspapers selling hearing aids. These ads are very expensive. I once talked to a person in the hearing aid industry, and he confided to me that an audiologist receives a $1,000. commission for each hearing aid he sells. Most people have two ears. So we are talking about a $2,000 commission for one pair of hearing aids!

Do you think the audiologist or his/her boss is interested in research into regeneration of the ear's inner nerves? I doubt it. It is possible that if the money were targeted on the nerves in ears, a simple injection or pill might replace the needs for all hearing aids!

I suggest that we the citizens learn how our tax dollars are being spent on research. Now.

Because America does not have a national healthcare program, 33% of women are unable to pay for birth control.

Consequently, America has a far higher non-voluntary pregnancy rate than other developed nations. There could be far less need for abortions if Americans had Medicare for All.

In conclusion for this chapter about Americans' lack of healthcare and food problems, I think you readers are constantly witnessing the connection between corporations and corruption in the USA. True Democracies do not have these problems. For clean government, you must stamp out collusion between corporations and government officials. There are nations that have caring governments, especially in Scandinavia (Denmark, Norway, Sweden, and Finland.) I strongly recommend studies be made of their laws and governmental agencies.

The next chapter will address political reform. I hope you will find it interesting and helpful in your quest for better government in your country. This chapter should provide you with some innovative tools to use in obtaining a honest and caring government.

POLITICAL REFORM AND MEDIA REFORM

"Money! Money! Money! - how it does do bad.
Ban it! Let man be,
so he can do good." …..H. Greenebaum

The foundation of good government is to assemble a group of men and women who are competent , caring, and clean.

The three Cs. Sounds easy. Unfortunately, it is not. We only have to look around the world to see how many governments lack all three Cs. So we must begin to search for answers. Because there are 7 billion of us on this planet, we can't just go our merry ways. We need government to build infrastructure so we can transport ourselves, food, and materials. We need government to make laws and regulations to protect us. We need governments to build schools for our children. And we need governments to give assistance to the disabled, the sick, the poor, and the unemployed. We need government to protect our planet. Yes, and we need good government.

We all need new ways to select our leaders and representatives in government. The present methods are not providing the right people. When I was active in US politics, I was astounded by the low levels of intellect, knowledge, morality, and sensitivity of American politicians. I suspect that the same problems exist elsewhere.

So, let's take one characteristic at a time. First, competence.

Should we allow just anybody to run our governments? Of course not. If we need a doctor, we want someone trained in the field of medicine. Since government officials face a diversity of problems emanating from diverse fields, perhaps we should divide government branches, and allow only candidates trained in a certain field to be elected to this branch.

For example, if one branch of the government covers agriculture, candidates should have degrees in agriculture, and hopefully experience as well. If one branch of government is foreign policy, we need worldly candidates who have degrees in diplomacy and experience in international matters. This differs completely from the way the American government is structured and the way candidates are selected. And we, American citizens, are now the victims of this incompetence.

As I ponder this new method of selection, I begin to wonder if we should leave this selection to voters.

Perhaps, it is time to question if elections are the answer to good government. After all, what really do voters know about the candidates? American elections do not attract candidates with expertise. They attract hustlers of money for campaigns who promise much and produce little. We have a preponderance of lawyers in the US governments. It is true that lawyers study laws, and a certain amount of them would certainly be needed in the process of law making, but I question the excess of people with this narrow a training.

So, for a starter, I believe we should require our government to be divided into several branches, and the candidates for public office, be required to apply their educational background and employment experience to a branch of government that relates to their expertise, if they have any.

There also is the question of how many people do we need in government? Does the USA really need 435 elected officials in the US House of Representatives? Does the USA really need 100 elected officials in the US Senate? It may be time to rethink how a revised government might be structured. 535 elected officials may not be the best number for efficiency and transparency.

Should we continue to give small states the same power as large states? Or should representation be by population alone?

These questions should be studied by all people in all nations, so all of us can design better governments to serve us more efficiently, and with far more transparency. We, the citizens, must be enabled to observe the workings of our governments with ease. The more transparency, the less corruption, and the more representation of the public interests.

The characteristic of caring is even more difficult to recognize in candidates.

In the past we voters are easily attracted to the guys who have the best smiles. We have been duped. Just because somebody is good at showing their teeth, is no reason to conclude that he/she is a caring person. First impressions are deceptive.

We voters need to learn how to examine candidates more deeply in order to determine if this person really cares about the safety of workers, wages of workers, unemployed workers, disabled persons, poor persons, children, the elderly, healthcare of citizens, civil rights, and oh yeah, the planet! We need thorough background checks of all candidates. We need to study their personnel files. We need psychological testing of candidates.

Why is caring so important in selection of candidates?

Because if you vote for candidates who are only interested in their own careers, you are exposing your country to cruel, insensitive governance that can be a disaster for all. The best example of this insensitivity was being played out right in front of us in July and August of 2011. The Tea Partiers and Republicans have pushed through a deficit plan that will smash Social Security for the elderly, Medicare for the elderly, and Medicaid for the poor. Their sole efforts were aimed at protecting their rich contributors from paying any taxes! They are backing the agenda for the super rich who have never supported any type of public program for the poor, the elderly, or for our children.

When we try to choose caring candidates, we are involved in choosing a certain type of government that we would be comfortable with and, yes, proud of. This is the core question that citizens must focus on. Today's America is rapidly changing from a caring government with public programs to a non-caring entity that caters to the rich and ignores the needs of the rest of the people.

And the last of the Cs is clean candidates.

By clean, I mean honest and unconnected to big money contributors. Because if they are already owned by big corporations, you are not going to be represented by this person. He/she is already in the other camp. He/she is already spoken for. They are not going to vote for your interests.

How do we identify an unclean candidate? Before we get smart and ban money from our elections, we must see who is funding their campaigns. See how much money they have "raised." In other words, "follow the money."

This is what has happened to American government. We allow our elections to be conducted like auctions, the highest bidders get the candidates.

And then the newly elected spend their entire career catering to their contributors. What a debacle!

"Don't Do What We Did" is a constant reminder to learn from our many mistakes, so your new governments will serve you much better.

In American elections, nothing is left to chance.

All candidates are flooded with questionnaires from big "contributors"/ bribesters. Candidates who want money answer the many questions on how they will vote on different issues. These questionnaires are then returned to the curious rich guys. They then interview the candidates, and take a careful look at the backgrounds of these new people. If they suspect that the candidate has a bit of principle or morality lurking back there somewhere, they are not selected.

You see, the "contributors" want stooges, robots, non-thinkers; in other words Republican storm troopers who march endlessly to the drum beats of their "contributors." That is why they supported people like George W. Bush and Ronald Reagan. They want "team players". Nauseating as it sounds, it is today's reality in US government. And the reach of money has not ignored members of the other side of the aisle, Democrats.

The tentacles of "contributors" has snared far, far too many Democrats, as well. The former party for the workers has forgotten their blue collar friends, and now focuses on solely staying in office. Democrats have failed to fight for principle too many times to be trusted anymore. Voters need a third party, a real Labor Party, that will represent the other 98%.

Today's America is big on guns.

They spent over half of all tax dollars on military spending and waging wars, both overt and covert. America can still be saved, but American citizens have got to become active in politics to stop the landslide into Fascism. Wow! I said it. Have you ever heard anybody suggest that America is becoming Fascist?

Well, let's examine what exactly is Fascism. I have a chart that was written by Laurence W. Britt, who researched 7 fascist regimes- Hitler's Germany, Mussolini's Italy, Franco's Spain, Salazar's Portugal, Papadopoulos's Greece, Pinochet's Chile, and Suharto's Indonesia.

Britt entitled this chart, "Early Warning Signs of FASCISM." Here are the warning signs. Compare them with what has happened in America and what is happening in your country:

#1 Powerful and continuing nationalism

#2 Disdain for Human Rights

#3 Identification of enemies as a unifying cause

#4 Supremacy of the military

#5 Rampant sexism

#6 Controlled mass media

#7 Obsession with national security

#8 Religion and government intertwined

#9 Corporate power protected

#10 Labor power suppressed

#11 Disdain for intellectuals and the arts

#12 Obsession with crime and punishment

#13 Rampant cronyism and corruption

#14 Fraudulent elections

Eerie isn't it? And all the time we Americans believed that we had democracy. You cannot have a green house if it is painted yellow. We Americans have become color blind. We have been losing our wonderful democracy, and have not even known it. Can we paint our house green again? Yes, if citizens take politics seriously and get active. And we have a lot of work to do.

Speaking of choosing candidates brings up today's methods of voting.

American elections are now conducted by electronic voting on machines. Is this better? Definitely not. It is very dangerous and unreliable. The voting machines are manufactured by private corporations who have refused to reveal the nature and details of the software in these machines. These machines have been examined by several experts and found to be very vulnerable to hacking and manipulation of the votes cast in them. Owners of the vote machine companies are strong supporters of the Republican party.

I, personally, refuse to vote on these machines, and choose to vote by paper ballot and to mail my votes back to the election agency. I believe this is imperative to having your vote being counted. I am also concerned about the vote counting machines used by the election agencies. I do not trust them either.

The safest way to get all votes counted honestly is to use paper ballots and hand count the cast ballots.

There should be video cameras directed at the vote counters, so we can detect any foul play. Frequent re-checks of counts should also be done so any deliberate miscounting can be quickly discovered and the crooked counter is arrested and taken off to jail. I have no sympathy with anybody who is trying to rig elections, and trying to give my votes to the bad guys. Police should be present at all counting of votes. Candidates and representatives of his/her party or campaign should be present to witness the counting.

Promoters of the vote machines, and bribed clerks from county election departments will argue that the vote counting will take too much time, but "that dog don't hunt".

There is no hurry to count votes. The only important element of any election is that the votes are counted honestly. If it takes 3 days, so be it. The organization of hand counting can be done with much less time than argued by lazy or bribed election officials.

I believe all votes should be cast by mail. The mailed in ballots should be delivered to a central location where a large amount of people are organized and trained in counting. All sorts of video cameras, police, and security should be present and well trained in advance of the arrival of the mail. Television should also be present to allow the public to monitor the whole process of counting. No machines should be involved in the counting. Just human eyes and hands.

We must restore public confidence to our elections. If we all vote by mail, we have more time to vote, do not lose time from work, cannot be victimized by bullies at polling places, and can avoid vote manipulation by machines or crooks at the polling places.

We should make sure there is plenty of security during the entire mailing process as well. Research should be done in advance of elections to determine how the hand counting of votes can be done accurately and quickly. The researchers can help determine the quantity of people needed to count the votes. The researchers can also concentrate on how to achieve the peak of integrity throughout the entire process, from the mailing of the ballots to the handling of the counts, so every vote counts.

These changes should provide a heightened excitement in voting and a large increase in confidence in government as the public views on their television the counts being posted for them to see.

Before voting, we need to prepare ourselves far more thoroughly than we have done in the past.

Because we will be voting by mail, we will have ample time to study the ballot measures and the candidates, far more in detail. We should ask questions and use our computers to research for even more details.

I believe that people of all nations should begin to seriously begin to discuss how to coordinate the remaking of all of our governments. The more deliberation and intense thinking together, the better we can all achieve balanced economies that allow all citizens to enjoy prosperity, have adequate healthcare, and have more joy during our short lifetimes.

Justice and fairness must be goals that we are striving for.

 Poverty must be eliminated right along with the elimination of hoarding of wealth by the 2% of the population. Non-violence must be the modus operandi. Revolution is not a consideration. We must organize and mobilize non-violent
demonstrations focused on peace and justice for all.

We must anticipate dirty tactics by the rich who want to desperately hang on to their excessive wealth.

We must make sure that all people understand that we are not trying to eliminate self improvement or entrepreneurialism. We respect people saving some money and building a nice home to live in. But we do not think people should be allowed to accumulate so much wealth that millions of workers' jobs and wages become the casualties of their hoarding of a finite quantity of wealth. This stress for economic balance and justice are the themes to project to the media.

We want the economies of every country to grow. They will be able to grow if more of their citizens are able to afford to buy houses, cars, clothing, etc. Poverty can be eliminated and people can become rich to a level that does not impact others. Hoarding hundreds of millions of dollars and billions of dollars is wrong.

A maximum accumulation of $10 million in assets or so must be discussed and agreed upon. We must all share so we can live in peace and comfort. Gee, that shouldn't be that difficult to understand. And we can accomplish this if citizens of all nations band together and work for the common good. Wars will be buried in history books. Peace is the primary goal of all. Declaration of neutrality and mass disarmament must be the goal of all thinking people. Violence should not be in our vocabulary.

We must sit down and examine what are our priorities.

Do we want to continue to fight wars all around the world? Do we want to continue to allow Congress people to accept bribes and shift taxes from rich individuals and corporations to our backs? Do we want our schools privatized, and only available to the rich ? Do we want Medicare for the elderly privatized? Do we want Medicaid for the poor smashed, so poor people have no more access to medical care? Do we want Social Security privatized and subject to huge losses on the Stock Market?
Do we want our government accepting bribes from corporations, and then rewarding them with tax breaks to send our jobs out of the country? (That's right, today, our government is rewarding corporations for outsourcing millions of American jobs to foreign lands.) And this is not just happening in America. In tiny little New Zealand the largest appliance manufacturer is sending its factories and jobs to poor countries, abandoning its workers in this far away nation.

All of the above is the agenda of many rich individuals and corporations.

It is time American citizens learned who is responsible for the decline of America. Selfishness and uncontrolled greed rule. Public interests are not on the table for consideration.

For those of you who are still smarting from the suggestion that America is becoming Fascist, here is news for you. On July 13, 2011 the NATION magazine and the Center for Media and Democracy revealed for the first time, the truth about an organization called ALEC, the American Legislative Exchange Council. This organization is a coalition of conservative elected state legislators in collusion with a very large group of American corporations.

The corporations contribute huge amounts of money to get their agenda passed. The state legislators meet in secret with representatives of corporations and actually VOTE IN SECRET on bills written by corporate lobbyists! *Corporate* donors have <u>veto power</u> over the language in the bills that are introduced in every state capitol in America! Please read that again. The last time I looked, I thought the President was the only official who has Veto power. "In this organization of conservative state legislators, the corporations have Veto power over the details in these bills that are being passed in states all over the country."

There have been hundreds of bills introduced in duplicate all around the country. Hundreds of these bills have been passed by bribed legislators! The documentation of ALEC has been publicized on the following web site for all to see how far we have gone from having a democracy . www.ALECexposed.org You will find a list of the corporations involved in this usurpation of our democracy. You will find a who's who of well known corporations on the Board of Directors of ALEC. And I am now going to list the true agenda of the rich. I believe you will find this agenda is a direct threat to most things that most of you believe in and want for your country.

#1 ALEC members have introduced bills to give tax breaks to corporations and cripple the states' ability to raise revenue, including rules limiting state taxing powers. ALEC bills attempt to privatize public programs. They do not want the state to have the power to regulate corporate activities. So, when you see school classrooms crowded with 50 students, instead of the planned 24, you will see what happens when the rich deprive your state of revenue to pay for teachers!

#2 ALEC members are pushing and pushing to privatize education, Medicare, Medicaid, public pension funds, social programs, prisons, and prison labor.

The privatization of public programs will sentence millions of people to poverty, and much shorter lifetimes. When a program is for-profit and no longer public, many people will lose access because the prices that include profits will be unaffordable. That is why over 51 million Americans, today, have no health insurance. They cannot afford it.

Meanwhile, citizens in France, Denmark, England, and all other industrialized nations offer a government run national healthcare program.

Thanks to a dishonest American media and bribed elected officials, Americans are dying by the thousand each year from lack of medical care. And it will get worse and worse as the Republicans attempt to privatize the few public programs available to the elderly, the severely disabled, children, the poor, and the unemployed.

#3 ALEC bills would repeal wage laws for workers, and encourage prison labor for corporations. ALEC bills support trade bills that move US factories and jobs out of the country.
American workers and their families are not considered in this cruel agenda of slashing the livelihood of millions of hard working Americans. The rich just don't care.

#4 ALEC bills are aimed at destroying labor unions. ALEC bills are designed to inhibit lawyers from filing law suits for consumers who have been injured or killed by dangerous products. I repeat, the rich just don't care.

#5 ALEC is pushing Voter ID legislation that requires all voters to present state photo identification to qualify to vote in elections.
This can hurt Democrats who are students, elderly, poor, and minorities. This is a dagger in the heart of American democracy!

#6 ALEC conservative legislators are encouraged to oppose any governmental position to raise wages. ALEC opposes expansion of healthcare to cover such afflictions as autism. ALEC opposes consumer protection legislation.
You now can see how US corporations have taken control of the US government in state capitols and in the national capitol in Washington. This is not what you should allow to happen in your country, and I hope Americans

will wake up and take back their government from corporations. A democracy is supposed to be for the people, not for the corporations. Fascism has, indeed, crept into America, and is now growing at a terrible pace.

I believe that America- now- needs a third party.

Because neither party is doing anything to help American workers! There is now a Great Depression for American workers. Every poll taken of US voters indicates a huge majority dislike both political parties. There has never been an opportunity for the success of a third party like now.

Most nations already have Labour parties that represent their workers. It is time for America to have a Labor Party. I suggest that all US labor unions get together fast, and persuade AL Gore to run as candidate for the Labor Party. . If it is too late for the Primary, get a national write-in campaign to elect Al Gore for President and Labor candidates for every position in Congress as well.

The public deserve representation.

They have none now. Bribery rules. It is time to kick out the crooks and get our Democracy back again. I suggest Al Gore because he has the experience of being a Vice President. He is a friend of the Environment. He has principles. He beat George Bush, but was cheated out of the Presidency by a crooked Supreme Court. We need justice back in our government.

The Internet with social networks should be harnessed to promote slogans like "No more outsourcing of our jobs!"

The people voted for " Change" when they elected Obama. And they got "change" all right. They lost their homes! And they lost their jobs! And interest rates went up on their credit cards! And health insurance premiums went up again and again!

Obama should have run as a Republican. He sure is not a Democrat. His decisions have all favored rich individuals, banks, and corporations. Give him to the Republicans. They can have him.

At this point in time, you might conclude that American government is not for sale any longer. It has already been sold to rich corporations and rich individuals. If you study the voting on bills with good names, but with bad stuff in the small print, you can see what happens when your government is staffed with incompetent, non-caring, and unclean elected officials.

America can be labeled the "most corrupt nation in the world"

Just add up the amount of bribes given to candidates for public office and the money given to them while they are in office. Follow their voting behaviour. Bribes keep flowing before they vote on bills, and after they vote on bills. The definition of bribery is " when a person in a position of public trust, accepts a gift of value, and allows this gift to affect his/her behaviour." This is precisely what "contributors" want to happen. They give money to a candidate's campaign so he/she will vote for their interest, and lo and behold, the candidate does vote for their interest.

Think for a moment. If the government was clean, why would anybody be giving millions of dollars to elected officials to vote their way?

Unless, their way was the wrong way, and was not going to benefit the public. Yes, money is given to divert votes from protecting the public. It is given to protect a few, at the cost of many.

Taxes are cut for the rich, and diverted to the backs of the hard working masses to pay. Medicare for All is blocked so health insurance companies can continue to choke the US economy with steadily increasing monthly premiums to the masses. Bank owned credit card companies in the USA are allowed to charge interest rates over 30% because a bribed Congress voted so, and President Obama signed the phony bill into law.

The solution is simple, and can be seen in effect in other countries that do care for their citizens.

Ban all money from outside interests in your elections. Treat money as the cancer of good government, and you will cure the ills of bad government. Also ban candidates from using their own money too. We do not want to allow rich candidates to buy elections, either. Elections must be conducted on level playing fields, so all candidates can compete fairly.

Elections must be funded equally from tax dollars.

It will be the best investment of tax dollars, by far, to buy clean elections. Every candidate must sign papers that allow a government agency to have access to all of his/her financial records. This agency must be empowered to charge officials with bribery charges if they find no evidence that the large amounts of money appearing on their bank statements, had a legitimate source. Trials will determine if the official is guilty of bribery. If convicted of bribery, the penalty must be adequate time spend behind bars in a prison.

We must be diligent about the prevention of bribery to our representatives. The US Constitution declares that bribery is a felony. It is time to enforce this part of the Constitution, and stop the flow of bribes to our elected officials. Contributions of any kind must be banned. No more money in our elections! PERIOD. Only our tax dollars must be allowed in our elections. Not too much to ask. So- ASK IT!

All of the above and below can form the blue print for clean government in any nation.

Do not allow money to contaminate your governmental elections.

There should be term limits on all elected offices, including the Supreme Court. Salaries should be lowered so people run to help their country, and not to help themselves. All terms of office should be for 4 years. No more 2 years for the House of Representatives and 6 years for the Senate, and no lifetime terms for Supreme Court judges. 4 years for all offices, period.

Next, we must consider the multi political party system that we are now saddled with. In August 2011 the US government had but 24 hours to meet a deadline to lift the budget level or to be unable to pay their mountains of bills. There had been a furious battle between the Republican and Democratic parties, on how to lower the Deficit. The Republicans defended rich individuals and corporations from any sort of taxes. The Democrats said they would protect public programs and then reversed their stand and totally capitulated to the Republicans. The problem with these two parties is that neither party will even consider listening to the numerous polls that have shown that the public wants taxes raised on rich individuals, corporations forced to pay taxes, and sharp cuts in military spending. It the public had its way, the budget could easily be managed. Both parties' decisions are based on catering to their rich contributors.

Since the US government is not sensitive to the wishes of the public, can it still be called a Democracy?

More on this in a few pages, but keep that question perking.

The actions by these two parties are not dictated by public interests, but are dictated by bribery. Neither party wants to lose its valued contributors. And another problem exists. The Republican party has allowed a bunch of fanatics called the Tea Party to gain control of their meager minds. The Tea Party is a recent phenomenon that began as a bunch of angry people who did not really know whom was responsible for the losses of their jobs, their savings, and the general malaise engulfing America.

The Koch brothers, who are worth over $50 billion, and are still hungry for more billions, seized the opportunity to harness this anger towards " big government" and away from themselves, and others, who are hoarding the riches of America. They hired experienced political manipulators to persuade the members of the Tea Party that the cause of all American problems is "big government." These manipulators are very skilled in moving large groups of uninformed people towards the goals of their employers- the Koch brothers, and their rich cohorts. So, in the 2010 elections, the Tea Party candidates won lots of seats from Democrats, and the Republicans regained control over the US House of Representatives.

The problem with the newly elected Tea Party people, is that most of them lack the knowledge or experience to make wise decisions.

This, combined, with the ongoing fierce competition between political parties is causing the US government to implode!

When I was running for public office, I attended lots of meetings, organized by my party, the Democrats.

I was privy to observing elected Democrats talking strategy about the coming elections. I was not happy with everything I heard. I knew Republicans valued the interests of their party over the interests of the country, but I naively believed that Democrats were beyond this warped behaviour. I was wrong. I heard Democrats mouthing the same rot.

This is what you readers must learn about the political party system. It can be at cross currents to the interest of your country. Elected officials have one guiding goal. To keep their jobs as long as they can. This translates into beating the opposing party and the candidates for their jobs. So what happens too often, is that the party in opposition will try and make the majority party fail in its pursuits.

The interests of the nation loses out under these conditions.

The motivation to win elections causes the opposition to sabotage the programs of the majority party. The majority party may lose the next election. The public has already lost.

I suggest that no party be allowed to gain too much power. One way to accomplish this would be to put a maximum on the number of seats that a party could win. For example, legislate that no party may occupy more than 20% of the seats in parliament. This would open the Parliament to proportional representation. In short, more parties that could represent more views on a subject. Discussions would be more valid, rather than if one party held the majority of votes, and debate was ignored.

It might also be tried without any political parties.

Individuals would run for election, representing a certain region of the country. These individuals would then work alongside other elected representatives and their peers might hold elections for higher positions within the government. Their work mates in Parliament would certainly know more about them than strangers voting with scant information. These are different ideas that you and your mates may experiment with in creating your new government for your nation, as well as American citizens working on revamping our broken government.

I strongly recommend that you select a committee to visit the Scandinavian countries to learn how their governments operate

Study how they hold elections, and how their social programs work for their citizens. Interview their citizens and ask them for ideas of how your new government should be created. Don't do what we did.

I believe that when people choose to make a new type government that they should start with creation of a new national constitution.

This constitution should be discussed by a group of educated persons with backgrounds of competence, integrity, and sensitivity to the needs of all kinds of people, all types of animals, and to the needs of a sustainable planet. I believe this conference of persons should be held for at least one month of consultations, and maybe much longer.

A constitution for a nation should be the foundation of beliefs that will help all citizens prosper, have good health, and be able to live in peace. Social programs should be chosen that will meet the needs of citizens, allow them to be educated, trained for certain vocations that they favor, and contribute to overall happiness for many. I truly believe that the imbalance of wealth and poverty should be directly addressed, and a far more caring economy be embraced for all people. There is no fair argument that can justify so much wealth in so few hands at the cost of so much poverty and suffering by so many.

I strongly recommend that each nation's constitution limits an individual's accumulation of wealth so that each person can expect to receive livable wages, which will enable them to have adequate shelter, an ability to clothe and feed their families, and have leisure time to play in the sunshine.

I also strongly advise you to include in your nation's new constitution, strong laws that require corporations to pay ample taxes, with strong enforcement of this law. Every government needs taxes to pay for many things. No corporation should be allowed to escape paying their share. All sorts of tax loopholes, exemptions, overseas tax havens, etc. should be banned.

If corporations threaten to move to another country, make laws that can put large tariffs on the products or services from these tax dodgers. This is another reason that citizens from all nations need to band together so there are no tax havens for cheats.

The American constitution was written by several men, but included some slave owners, and lacked granting equal rights to females.

The conference finished the construction of the constitution on September 17, 1787. On March 4, 1789, a convention of state governments recommended that a group of 12 amendments be added to the constitution. The states expressed a desire, "in order to prevent misconstruction or abuse of its powers, that further declaratory and restrictive clauses should be added: And as extending the ground of public confidence in the Government , will best ensure the beneficent ends of its institutions"

On September 25, 1789 Congress sent the 12 amendments to the state legislatures, requiring ratification by three fourths of the states. Ten of the 12 amendments were ratified. These 10 amendments are called the Bill of Rights. They were ratified effective December 15, 1791.

As you can see the construction of a constitution, and needed changes takes time.

And, these 10 amendments have been debated over and over again with different opinions of their meanings. So, another lesson is to make the wording clear and easy to understand.

Let's take a look at Amendment # 1 :

"Congress shall make no law respecting an establishment of religion, or prohibiting the free exercise thereof; or abridging the freedom of speech, or of the press; or the right of the people peaceably to assemble, and to petition the Government for a redress of grievances."

Above is the exact wording. I will now declare my observations. The protection of different religions has been selective. Some branches of Christian religions have consistently tried to push their beliefs on to the Government. Others have not. Certain government officials have spoken negatively of the Moslem religion. Since there are 1.4 billion Moslems in the world, these officials have gravely injured the image of America to a very large population.

The freedom of speech of anti-war advocates has been encroached upon more and more frequently by the Government.

Recently, over 2,000 households have been invaded by the FBI with fraudulent interpretations of another poorly written law about "aiding and abetting terrorists." These people have lost their protections from the US Constitution to "peaceably assemble and to petition the Government for a redress of grievances." These actions by the FBI are very similar to the same acts perpetrated in   Fascist nations. The FBI's actions violate the above quoted First Amendment. How can this be happening in a Democracy?

The actions of our military in foreign nations by breaking down doors of homes of civilians is an extension to the domestic acts by the FBI. Americans must rein in these violations of the US Constitution, and get the country back on the track of Democracy.

I do not believe our military should be allowed to act against the US Constitution on foreign soil.

I believe all people of all nations should be treated with respect and fairly during wartimes or peace times.

I believe the American public should engage in open debate about the decisions to wage war, the manner that we behave during a war, such as bombing cities, using nuclear weapons, engaging in torture, etc.

I do not believe most Americans are even aware of the atrocities perpetrated by the US military and the CIA around the world.

The kidnapping of people, taking them to secret prisons around the world, and torturing them is not my idea of how a democracy is supposed to be behaving. The fear of another terrorist attack on America has turned the US democracy into a lawless nation afflicted with a severe case of paranoia.

If Americans truly value the principles of a free democracy that respects the rights of all peoples, they must come to grips with the actual behaviour of all of the components of our military.

I doubt if most Americans realize that we now maintain a secret striking force of over 60,000 men.

The overall organization is called SOCOM, (US Special Operations Command). The SOCOM was organized in 1987. SOCOM carries out secret missions which include assassinations, counterterrorist raids, long range reconnaissance, intelligence analysis, foreign troop training, and weapons of mass destruction counter-proliferation operations. SOCOM now receives $9.8 billion per year. So, this is not a small operation. It is quite large and quite frightening.

One of the components of SOCOM is called JSOC. (Joint Special Operations Command).

The primary mission of JSOC is to track and kill suspected terrorists. JSOC reports to the US President and acts under his authority. They maintain a global hit list which includes American citizens! There is a network of secret prisons around the world , used for "interrogation" alias torture. If they were legitimate prisons, they would not be secret! SOCOM is operating in at least 70 nations around the world! According to the former chief of SOCOM, Navy Admiral Eric Olson, *all of these secret operations are as a result of each nation's invitation.*

The problems with such a large operation of secret killings and kidnappings are enormous. How are we to distinguish between real terrorists planning to bomb America, and a dictator or president or a king desiring to eliminate a political opponent, an anti- war activist, an environmentalist trying to stop a corporation from polluting, or a group of people trying to change their government from fascist to democratic?

In other words, are most of these secret units killing good guys?

How would they know who is good or bad? Somebody identifies somebody as bad in their country, and requests a secret force from the USA to assassinate these people. Are we really killing bad people or good people? Think of it. We have 60,000 people in SOCOM! JSOC is operating as the President's private assassination squad. When did the President become God and Judge of the earth?

What right has any head of state, to order assassinations around the world?

And on such a grand scale! Admiral Olson, at a recent meeting at the Aspen Institute's Security Forum, stated that " a DOZEN or so black operations are conducted EVERY NIGHT! For those Americans who believe that all of this is necessary to protect them from another terrorist attack, I believe they need to take a pill.

These nightly raids around the world are not protecting you, folks.

They are creating hatred for America! What right has any one nation to send secret assassination forces around the world to kill people? Are there not laws in every nation to arrest and charge criminals in a court. Who gave America the right to judge and condemn criminals, without a trial, to corporal punishment? We are now the world's largest executioners of so called bad guys. I think this stinks, and smells like the lynch mobs in the deep South, that hung innocent negroes from trees because somebody accused them of a crime that probably was perpetrated by a white person. I am highly suspect of the persons in other nations directing our hit teams at supposed terrorists.

As we have already learned, some US elected officials will accept bribes to keep their jobs. It is just one more step or two to consider employing some of our specially trained military to kidnap some troublesome American dissenters and fly them off to some secret prison for "interrogation".

This is exactly what was done in Argentina in the 1970s.

Thousands of Argentine citizens "disappeared" into secret prisons where they were tortured and murdered by their own government! These people were labor leaders, community organizers, activists, intellectuals, and lots and lots of dissenters. These people were just like you and me. It happened in Germany, too. It can happen in any nation that has lost its democracy and become Fascist.

Want a free vacation to an exotic country, try our "Rendition holiday". Send your application to the CIA in Washington, DC, USA.

The passage of the US Patriot Act opened the doors to legally arrest any persons falsely accused of suspicious activity, and deprive them of all legal rights, including due process. This law was passed after the 9/11 attacks on the USA. It is still in effect 10 years later! Americans are at risk with this loose weapon against civil rights lying open to temptation. You, an American citizen, can be falsely accused, and victimized to a Rendition kidnapping, secret imprisonment , and condemned to endless bouts of torture!

No nation, including the USA, should ever pass laws that deprive anyone of their legal rights to trial before judgment.

And as I said before, I believe America should be held accountable for our activities across our borders as well. I do not think any nation should ever be allowed to kidnap, torture, or execute anyone anywhere. Yes, you can arrest a person alleged to have committed a crime, but war or no war, everybody is entitled to an open trial, not some secret trial without a lawyer to defend you.

There should be strict laws prohibiting kidnapping people and taking them out of a country and placing them in secret prisons. This is exactly what the Germans did to the Jews! And they killed millions in secret prisons. America must be forced to become a law abiding nation again.

In 1776, the revolutionaries who rebelled against the English in America, could have been accused of being terrorists by the English.

 It is so easy to demonize others and accuse them of being bad, when in reality, many are just trying to gain their freedom from an unjust regime of government. All media in all countries should be more careful how they label people struggling for their freedom, and economic justice.

The media has labeled people acting as insurgents- the bad guys. I do not think some of the media even knows the definition of an insurgent. An insurgent is a person who is revolting against a given authority. As we all know some of the authorities of countries are not nice guys. They are killing people who are fighting for their freedoms. Just as American citizens fought for their freedoms from the English. Insurgents are a threat to authority. These authorities welcome American secret forces coming in to kill the leaders of the trouble makers. But do American citizens really want $ 9.8 billion of their tax dollars spent killing people fighting for their freedom and independence from unjust and often cruel leaders? Whose side are we on ? Each American administration claims that it is trying to spread democracy around the world. If so, why are we allowing cruel governments to invite our hit teams to come over and assassinate leaders of the insurgency, and train the armies of dictators to kill insurgents?

It is important that we all learn what is the score here.

We need to help Americans overcome their fears of terrorists, and stop this madness of slaughtering freedom seeking insurgents. There is much work to be done. Let's all get involved.

I am sure dishonest leaders of lots of countries are waiting in line to accuse unhappy citizens who are demonstrating against their administration, of being terrorists. Why not? The Americans do not have to abide by any laws that would stop these secret killings and kidnappings. They are eager to please. Folks, this can and may already be happening in your country. We need people from all over the world to stand up and stop America from committing any more of these heinous crimes against mankind.

We need your help. I can assure you that most Americans do not know anything about these secret raids, and have no idea of the scope.

Remember, America has 308 million citizens. Most of them are honest, hard working people just like you. It only takes a few to taint the many. I am hopeful that the American public will learn about these attacks, and demand that they stop. I hope the American readers arouse their neighbors of these unwarranted activities and show the courage to demand a halt to these programs.

We cannot maintain we are a democracy, and allow our fears to justify such activities. We must learn that justice and respect for all peoples is the only defense against terrorists. These secret raids are not secret to the families of these victims. America is creating terrorists out of the victims of our unjustified attacks on their loved ones. Violence begets violence. You cannot expect otherwise from these acts of violence. It is time to teach the causes of terrorism to American voters and teach them how America can regain its democracy, by practicing the principle of justice for all.

The so called wars in Afghanistan, Iraq, and Pakistan have included thousands of nightly US special operations raids, and bombings by unmanned drones. The CIA who direct the drones' attacks deny that any civilians have been killed by the drones. This statement dies in the faces of the many families who have lost loved ones to the "dreadful" Americans. That is the mildest description of their feelings manufactured by the hands of CIA operators and other US military forces.

BACK TO THE CONSTITUTION

Even with these 10 amendments, it took America 74 more years , and a civil war, to finally free the slaves! It took 129 years and the passage of the 19th amendment to finally allow females to vote in America!

And, today, 224 years after the passage of the US Constitution, we do not have *freedom of the press*.

The American press is owned and dominated by a handful of big corporations who are not bashful in how they control it. American elections are definitely affected by a press that has not chosen to be neutral in elections. They openly endorse candidates in many elections.

They do not treat candidates in a fair and impartial manner. They definitely have their favorites. This is not the way a democracy should be operating. The English have created the BBC to provide their citizens with impartial coverage. The English also have several newspapers that a voter has a choice to read. This is not the case in most American cities. Most US cities today have only one major daily newspaper to read.

In New Zealand where I now live, there is only one major daily newspaper to read, and their coverage of candidates is very biased.

Their favorite for Prime Minister is John Key of the National Party. The leader of the Labour Party is Phil Goff. When they publish photos of these two major candidates, the photo of John Key shows him in full stature. The photo of Phil Goff is only of his head and is much, much smaller. The newspaper is always quick to find fault with Phil Goff, once running large articles about Goff coloring his gray hairs darker. This was supposed to be important news. How many people do you know color their hair? Especially females. Is this some kind of bad thing that should be in headlines? Unless, you want the opposition leader to look bad.

It is time that the Press is required to maintain a neutral position in elections.

Their independence is not justified, when they have a monopoly of the important coverage of elections. The Press should not be allowed to manipulate any nation's election coverage.

As we all know, Rupert Murdoch owns a lot of newspapers and television news shows. And his news outlets have been charged with hacking into all types of people's private emails, giving bribes to police, favoring certain politicians, etc. The bottom line is that we citizens should not allow rich people and rich corporations to dominate our media.

We need a media that we can trust and will give us accurate and impartial news.

Every nation should severely restrict the ownership of all branches of media to tiny percentages of the industry. And this includes publishing companies as well. In order to have a free press and book publishing industry, authors and journalists need to be able to think freely and express their opinions and ideas in books and in newspapers without a huge overpowering corporation dictating their agenda into the writers' minds. That is not free press. We must demand the end of monopolies controlling our media.

A prime example of how mass media distorts the news is the media's handling of Climate Change.

The media has allowed lying scientists paid by oil, gas, and coal companies to have equal press coverage with the thousands of scientists around the world screaming warnings to all of us to stop the pollution before the world becomes unable to stop the acceleration of Climate Change. The liars have been allowed to drown out the dire warnings from sincere and honest scientists.

Bribed governmental officials have distorted the findings of the scientific world. Our planet is in severe trouble. We had snow in Auckland, New Zealand on August 15, 2011! That is the first time in 72 years people there have even seen a snow flake. Aug. 15, 2011 was the coldest day recorded in the history of Auckland, the largest city in New Zealand! All over the world we are witnessing bizarre behaviour in our weather. Folks, Climate Change is here.

It will get much worse if we continue to allow paid propagandists to distort the facts. These people are being paid to lie so their employers can continue to sell the items that are causing Climate Change. The fuels of fools are oil, gas, and coal. These fossil fuels are destroying our planet.

The media should not be allowed to give equal coverage to people who would take money to declare that the planet is flat. Enough of the liars. Enough of a media, bribed by advertising, giving voices to flat earthers.

We have got a very, very serious problem.

It is time to prioritize directing our tax dollars away from wars, away from subsidies to oil companies(yes, oil companies are still receiving tax subsidies while making tens of billions of dollars in profits!), and towards building alternate clean sources of energy, such as solar and wind. *Time is running out.*

The "freedom of speech" rights have been manipulated by US corporations' lawyers to include corporations as having these personal rights.

Several Supreme Court decisions have tilted towards corporations, and against public interests. Certain members of the US Supreme Court have become quite cozy with the wealthy, and quite isolated from the needs of the public. The decision to stop the recount of votes, when Al Gore was leading in total votes, gave the Presidency to George W. Bush!

When the US Constitution was written in 1787, few people lived beyond the age of 50. So, the Constitution granted lifetime terms for members of the Supreme Court! We now have a deeply entrenched Supreme Court of conservatives who vote for corporations' welfare instead of the people's welfare. Don't Do It Like We Did It. Do not give anyone a lifetime term in anything. It will boomerang against the public interests. The American public should demand that lifetime terms be abolished, and short terms be substituted. There is certainly no shortage of lawyers and judges in the USA!

The present Supreme Court has voted to legalize uncontrolled political contributions by corporations in elections, and also voted to allow uncontrolled political contributions by foreign people or foreign corporations in US elections!

And the same Supreme Court has eliminated the requirements to disclose the names of the contributors. In essence, the US Supreme Court has expanded the acts of bribery to new heights of corruption in a so called democracy that is now controlled by rich corporations and rich individuals.

I believe the more citizens who gather together from all nations to rewrite their national constitutions, the better will be the brotherhood to strive for prosperity and peace for all nations.

I believe that there should be conferences on the waging of wars, and how to put an end to wars.

These conferences should promote nations to declare neutrality. And this neutrality includes the end of funding for weapons of war. This neutrality should require all governments to abide by international courts that are given the power to arrest and try war criminals. The sales of arms to other nations should be declared illegal. Bombing of cities should be declared illegal. Possession of nuclear weapons should be declared illegal. It is time to get serious about peace. It has been much too easy to get serious about waging wars. Let's all turn our energy toward peace, and justice for all peoples.

The recent riots in England by the poor and unemployed is similar to the race riots in the USA in the 1960s. They are both the desperate acts by masses of unrepresented citizens. They have been ignored. Their voices have been silenced. The present tilted economies toward the rich and away from the working people is cruel and uncaring for the needs of the many.

The unemployment rates for youths is much, much higher than for other ages.

The priorities of governmental spending is tilted away from the needs for young people. College tuitions have sky rocketed, so most families will be unable to send their children to higher educational institutions. This is wrong. Conservatives who do not believe in helping anyone, have taken control of lots of governments. They do not support financial aid for college students. They do not believe in government grants for poor students to attend college. They are only interested in privatizing all institutions so they can make more money. They are balancing budgets on our children's backs.

They have no compunctions to cutting the taxes of corporations. And they have no compunctions on cutting the funds for educations of our children. This needs to be reversed. People have got to wake up to the real agendas of the rich. They do not care for you and me. They do not want to pay taxes to make life better for the public. They are selfish and the sooner we change things around to a caring world, the better.

As in all generalizing, there are always exceptions. On August 14, 2011, the second richest American, Warren E. Buffett, issued a statement that deserves important attention.

I believe it is so important, I am going to print his exact words. And I also believe Mr. Buffett's statement is very, very important support to my recommendation for a maximum wage that will strongly contribute toward vitally needed balanced economies around the world.

Here is Mr. Buffett's complete statement:

"Our leaders have asked for 'shared sacrifice'. But when they did the asking, they spared me. I checked with my mega-rich friends to learn what pain they were expecting. They, too, were left untouched.

While the poor and middle class fight for us in Afghanistan, and while most Americans struggle to make ends meet, we mega-rich continue to get our extraordinary tax breaks. Some of us are investment managers who earn billions from our daily labors but are allowed to classify our income as 'carried interest,' thereby getting a bargain 15 percent tax rate. Others own stock index futures for 10 minutes and have 60 percent of their gain taxed at 15 percent, as if they had been long-term investors.

These and other blessings are showered upon us by legislators in Washington who feel compelled to protect us, much as if we were spotted owls or some other endangered species. It's nice to have friends in high places.

Last year my federal tax bill- the income tax I paid, as well as payroll taxes paid by and on my behalf-was $ 6,938,744.That sounds like a lot of money. But what I paid was only 17.4 percent of my taxable income-and that's actually a lower percentage than was paid by any of the 20 other people in our office. Their tax burdens ranged from 33 percent to 41 percent and averaged 36 percent.

If you make money with money, as some of my super-rich friends do, your percentage may be a bit lower than mine. But if you earn money from a job, your percentage will surely exceed mine-most likely by a lot.

To understand why, you need to examine the sources of government revenue. Last year about 80 percent of these revenues came from personal income taxes and payroll taxes. The mega-rich pay income taxes at a rate of 15 percent on most of their earnings but pay practically nothing in payroll taxes. It's a different story for the middle class; typically, they fall into the 15 percent and 25 percent income tax brackets, and then are hit with heavy payroll taxes to boot.

Back in the 80s and 90s, tax rates for the rich were far higher, and my percentage rate was in the middle of the pack. According to a theory I sometimes hear, I should have thrown a fit and refused to invest because of the elevated tax rates on capital gains and dividends.

I didn't refuse, nor did others. I have worked with investors for 60 years and have yet to see anyone- not even when capital gains rates were 39.9 percent in 1976-77- shy away from a sensible investment because of the tax rate on the potential gain. People invest to make money, and potential taxes have never scared them off. And to those who argue that higher rates hurt job creation, I would note that a net of nearly 40 million jobs were added between 1980 and 2000. You know what's happened since then: lower tax rates and far lower job creation.

Since 1992, the I.R.S. has compiled data from the returns of the 400 Americans reporting the largest income. In 1992, the top 400 had aggregate taxable income for $ 16.9 billion and paid federal taxes of 29.2 percent on that sum. In 2008, the aggregate income of the highest 400 had soared to $ 90.9 billion- a staggering $227.4 million on average- but the rate paid had fallen to 21.5 percent.

The taxes I refer to here include only federal income tax, but you can be sure that any payroll tax for the 400 was inconsequential compared to income. In fact, 88 of the 400 in 2008 reported no wages at all, though every one of them reported capital gains. Some of my brethren may shun work but they all like to invest. (I can relate to that.)

I know well many of the mega-rich and, by and large, they are very decent people. They love America and appreciate the opportunity this country has given them. Many have joined the Giving Pledge, promising to give most of their wealth to philanthropy. Most wouldn't mind being told to pay more in taxes as well, particularly when so many of their fellow citizens are truly suffering.

Twelve members of Congress will soon take on the crucial job of rearranging our country's finances. They've been instructed to devise a plan that reduces the 10-year deficit by at least $ 1.5 trillion. It's vital, however, that they achieve far more than that. Americans are rapidly losing faith in the ability of Congress to deal with our country's fiscal problems. Only action that is immediate, real and very substantial will prevent that doubt from morphing into hopelessness. That feeling can create its own reality.

Job one for the 12 is to pare down some future promises that even a rich America can't fulfill. Big money must be saved here. The 12 should then turn to the issue of revenues. I would leave rates for 99.7 percent of taxpayers unchanged and continue the current 2 percentage-point reduction in the employee contribution to the payroll tax. This cut helps the poor and the middle class, who need every break they can get.

But for those making more than $ 1 million- there were 236,883 such households in 2009- I would raise rates immediately on taxable income in excess of $ 1 million, including, of course, dividends and capital gains. And for those who make $ 10 million or more- there were 8,274 in 2009- I would suggest an additional increase in rate.

My friends and I have been coddled long enough by a billionaire - friendly Congress. It's time for our government to get serious about shared sacrifice."

I admire some of the thoughts of Mr. Buffett. However, his statement needs to be examined in more detail.

He stated that the "Job one for the 12 is to pare down some future promises… and Big money must be saved here." I suspect he is referring to Social Security, Medicare, and Medicaid. Yes, that is big money, but it is the pensions of the masses, and the healthcare of the masses. And the funding should be increased, not cut severely. Mr. Buffett says nice things, but he does not understand that cuts for these programs will result in the deaths of hundreds of thousands of people from hunger and disease! Social programs in far less rich countries such as France and the Scandinavian nations are funded much more generously than in America!

He also supports the 2% cut in payroll taxes. This cut will come back to haunt all the people who depend on Social Security. There should never be cuts in the revenue for Social Security. This cut is propagandized as a "tax holiday". It is pure BS. The creators of this phony tax cut are really trying to sabotage Social Security's financial base. The answer from the public should be " Keep your hands off my Social Security. Cut military spending. Raise taxes on the rich."

Mr. Buffett neglects to target the corporations who are making billions of dollars in profits and pay no taxes!

He neglects to suggest that America is spending trillions of dollars in wars, and this should be targeted immediately for cuts, instead of the promised pensions and healthcare of the elderly, the severely disabled, and the poor.

Mr. Buffett praises his rich friends for promising to give most of their wealth to charities. I say, promises are easily forgotten. The so called caring for "fellow citizens who are truly suffering" is NOW, not years from now. People are losing their houses to crooked banks who are once again forging names on documents and stealing houses from mortgage paying citizens. Buffett's friends are outsourcing more jobs across our borders than they are creating jobs on our soil. How about actions instead of false promises – NOW. Stop firing American workers! Stop trying to crush unions, and stop lowering the wages of hard working Americans.

I know Mr. Buffett is a whiz at numbers.

So, how can he talk about raising taxes on the rich, and in the same statement say, " leave the rates for the 99.7 percent of taxpayers unchanged." The last time I looked, the top 2 percent of the USA had immense shares of the total wealth and income, in comparison to the remaining 98 percent. Come on Warren, whose side are you on?

Mr. Buffett also stated that the rich "love America."

I would be interested in what part of America they love. They certainly don't love the people of America. Since they are firing American workers by the millions and moving their jobs overseas, and sentencing their families to poverty. They certainly don't love the air, water, trees, and land of America. Since their corporations are always trying to eliminate environmental regulations so they can freely pollute and poison our air, water, and soil. They certainly don't love democracy. Since many of the CEOs of America are members of ALEC where their high paid lobbyists are voting with their bribed state legislators to privatize all public programs, destroy the financial structure of states and schools, and destroy the structure of the federal government as well.

So what is left?

Maybe what they really love is to exploit American workers by attacking their unions so they can take away their benefits and lower their wages. Maybe what they really love is to pay themselves huge salaries, give themselves millions of dollars in stock options, and to steal homes with illegal foreclosure processes. Maybe what they really love is how they have managed to bribe the whole Republican party and most of the Democratic party so they can get tax cuts, deregulation, and lots of other goodies. I don't think these people should wear American flags in their lapels. They are traitors to America.

The USA now has over 900 military bases around the world!

I recommend that no nation be allowed to have any military bases on any other nation's soil or water. We need a strong United Nations military force that can stop any nation from waging war on any other nation. The UN military force must not be dominated by any one or more nations. Nobody voted for the USA to be the world's policeman. No nation should be allowed to dominate over others.

Individual nations should be encouraged to abandon spending huge sums of money for armies, navies, and air forces. Wars are profitable for defense contractors. They are not profitable for the public. The next war will be a threat to our entire planet. The idea of stopping wars is not an idealistic dream. It is the reality of extinction of the human race by nuclear warfare. Yes, indeed, we can do it now. We can destroy a whole world with the weapons of mass destruction.

And the knowledge of manufacturing nuclear weapons is no longer a secret. More and more nations are able to make and use nuclear weapons. Bombs that can destroy millions of people are here and now. We must use our brains and learn how to live in peace. We must destroy all nuclear weapons before they destroy us.

Nuclear war is an external threat to all citizens.

An internal threat to all citizens is the loss of representation of public interests because of corruption within our governments. We must garner the power of the masses to overcome these distortions of good government. We must use all forms of communication to educate the masses on how to regain control of their governments. We must emphasize the necessity to restrain all types of violence.

We need to mobilize working people in all nations to combine our efforts so we can gain balanced economies for all people.

We must explain to all peoples that this is a universal movement that will produce prosperity where there never was a presence of it before. We must build up hope for people who have been exploited for generations by selfish individuals and ruthless corporations.

We need to pass laws that protect organizers from a history of violence, paid for by corporations trying to stop labor organizing.

The steelworkers' unions of the USA and Mexico recently have been successful in helping each other mobilize against exploitation of workers. We need to expand this intelligent approach to securing international economic justice.

If we succeed in raising wages in all countries, American corporations will no longer be able to exploit the poor and motivated to laying off US workers. And if we succeed in raising wages in every nation, this will result in the expansion of consumer markets in every nation. This added spending will provide prosperity to many who have never dreamed this possible.

An enlightened world will finally learn how to share prosperity on a level far beyond present circumstances.

Instead of a few billionaires and millionaires, there will be a huge middle class that will have achieved financial security.

Social programs will be strengthened as the increased wages of many provide a new source of funding for better healthcare, better shelter, better food, better clothing, better transportation, etc.

Unemployment will be a word that has no more use in a world of balanced economies.

Parity of wages will be an international theme for all workers. Excessive wages to CEOs will be another past chapter in history. CEOs' salaries must never again be allowed to exceed a worker's by such huge ratios. Yes, leaders in industry who have advanced education and successful backgrounds in business leadership deserve more pay than those of us with less skills. But that pay must not be at a level that impinges on the welfare of workers and stock shareholders. Nobody is worth millions of dollars in salary per year. They just ain't that smart.

In August 2011, an Asian Development Bank study warned the citizens of Asia to address the problems of rising inequality, poor governance, corruption, and especially Climate Change.

These are the very same issues you have just read about in this book. They must be addressed worldwide. Here is a snapshot of how bad it is in the USA:

1% of Americans control 40% of its wealth! 1% of Americans receive 25% of the nation's total income! America's downslide is certainly related to this giant tilt upward of its wealth. This inequality of income and wealth has been growing exponentially in the USA, as well as around the world. It must be stopped! The impetus for change will certainly not come from the top. You- the victims of an unbalanced economy have work to do. We are talking about the future of your children!

All of the material in this book can be condensed into the description, " The Great Disconnect."

 Americans have lost their connection to their government – due to bribery. Americans have lost their individual freedoms and democracy – due to corporations taking control of their government. Americans have lost their healthcare – due to the greed of health insurance companies. Americans have lost their individual prosperity – due to the corruption of banks and their collusion with a bribed Congress. Americans have lost so much because they have not paid attention to politics. A democracy requires its defense by an informed and active populace. When the cat's away, the mice play! (I suggest that we substitute "rats" for "mice"- for many reasons.)

LEARN! EDUCATE! MOBILIZE! ACTION!

"Demonstrations get brief attention, and then the media turns the page.

Demonstrations get even less attention when you've lost your democracy. We must mobilize internationally and commit ourselves to a journey towards victory, for our children, and all children." ....H Greenebaum

We are now entering pages in history that have never been written before.

These new conditions demand new solutions that are bold and deliberately aimed at removing the lids off old attitudes.

You, the readers, can contribute far more to these changes than any generation before you ever dreamed of. Instead of inventing fancier mobile phones and other electronic gimmickry, you can produce economies that will raise billions of people from poverty. You can be responsible for securing job stability for all. You can. You really can. And now let's see how.

The four steps to implement change are –
LEARN - EDUCATE – MOBILIZE – ACTION

Photocopy the cover of this book and give it to friends so they will be able to remember the name of the book when they go to buy it. Tell them that there is definitely hope for all people on this planet.

Once we have shared this information, it is time to mobilize. My recommendation is to create a Labour Party in every nation, and be sure that these parties accept and work toward the same goals:

Goal #1
Equal wages across all borders, ending the exploitation of the poor, and ending the destructive practice of outsourcing jobs and factories. If all wages are equally high, all economies will enjoy strong growth. This will end the ruthless "race to the bottom" by narrow thinking CEOs.

Goal # 2
The Labour Party should concentrate on passing a law that creates a Maximum Wage income and Maximum Asset possession. I suggest a max income of $500,000. per year and a maximum accumulation of $ 10 million in assets. This can be accomplished by a change in taxation that bans hoarding of resources. The funds received by this more equitable distribution of wealth can be used to hire more teachers, rebuild the infrastructure, fund a Medicare for All Americans, pay for research for safe energy, etc.

Goal # 3
Criminalize pollution, so CEOs are held responsible for the destruction of our planet. No more phony cap and trade paper trades. If you dirty my air and water, you go to jail. PERIOD. We must protect our planet, and stop the destruction of the whole eco system.

Goal #4
Promote Neutrality for all nations, and organize regional UN military forces to combat any war- like activities by rogue nations. Destroy all weapons of mass destruction. Divert the huge defense expenditures to peace industries that can provide safe sources of energy. Push our governments to ban manufacturing of gasoline fuelled cars. Demand the government transition war industries into constructive industries that contribute toward the welfare of all peoples.

Goal # 5
Demand that the Labour Party provide social welfare programs that help the sick, the disabled, the minorities, the youths, and all who need help. Build up public programs, such as public schools, social security for the elderly, access to healthcare, and other various social services.

Goal # 6
Demand that the Labour Party bans all political contributions to candidates and to elected officials. Demand that the Labour Party legislates term limits

for all officials. Demand that all campaigns for public office be funded with tax dollars and each candidate receives equal sums.

Goal # 7

Demand that the Labour Party represents all working people, and represents the goals of environmentalists, anti-war advocates, and other groups working for worthy social goals. The Labour Party must be the stanchion of morality and principled goals.

You, the readers, must think and plan globally so our goals can be gained and retained. Citizens of all nations must work for the same goals with their Labour Parties. We must standardize our goals so it is easy for citizens to achieve these goals together, across all borders.

This global thinking will stop rogue corporations from finding tax havens to escape paying taxes to fund the social programs of their countries. This will stop corporations from escaping environmental regulations by moving their factories to a nation with a bribed government. We must have uplifting regulations for all nations on all aspects of behaviour . No more selling of worthless so called securities to unsuspecting customers in other nations. Strict regulations in all nations will protect us from swindlers and fraudsters.

We must use high tech procedures to spread these noble goals to all peoples. We now have the communication technology to spread this information rapidly. We must arm ourselves with facts, so crooks cannot deceive us.

America does not have a Labour Party. They need one – fast

They need to create a Labour Party with the above goals and get this party registered in every state for the upcoming elections. I recommend that they persuade Al Gore to run as their presidential candidate, and persuade Ralph Nader to run as Al Gore's Vice President. That would be an unbeatable combo.

We must all pay far more attention to politics and politicians. We must demand transparency, so we can monitor what they are doing with our tax dollars.

Lobbyists must be banned from the halls of all levels of governments.

Any hint of bribery must be investigated and the perpetrators charged and arrested. Corporations must be banned from all hints of interference with OUR GOVERNMENT. It is not theirs. We do not have to tolerate any attempts at control of a government which is meant for our protection. Never, never let corporations rule again in your country or mine. Enough.

The ball is now in your court.

I have finished my writing efforts to help you regain ownership of your governments and restore your freedoms. I will be rooting for you to succeed. Once you begin to work together with citizens from other nations, you will begin to taste victory for all. This must be a real team effort.

Best regards to all peoples.

Howard M Greenebaum, author

REFERENCES

Center for Public Integrity
Citizens for Tax Justice
CommonDreams.org
Cornucopia Institute
Earthjustice.org
Environmental Defense Fund EDF
Environmental Health News
Environmental News Network ENN
Environmental Working Group EWG
Friends of the Earth International
Institute for Public Accuracy
MoveOn.org
New Zealand Herald newspaper
New York Times
Off the Charts / Center on Budget & Policy Priorities
Public Citizen
Roots Action
TDC The Daily Climate
Washington Post

Book References

Many of these books were inspirational and thought provoking, and contributed to the opening of my mind to produce solutions. The books on Emerson, especially, raised my thinking levels, and also introduced me to a rhythm in writing. The books by Mahatma Gandhi helped me relate economics to humanity. All of these books combined to help me address the diversity of subjects that I have addressed. As a small business man I have had many years of performing a myriad of tasks. As a political problem solver, I have expanded my knowledge seeking to the many areas that impact our present lives, and to the future of mankind.

List of books by category

The Portable Emerson- Edited by Carl Bode. In collaboration with Malcolm Cowley
The Selected Letters of Ralph Waldo Emerson – Edited by Joel Myerson
Emerson, The Mind on Fire - by Robert D. Richardson, Jr.
Economic and Industrial Life and Relations, Volume I – by M.K. Gandhi
Economic and Industrial Life and Relations, Volume II – by M.K. Gandhi
Economic and Industrial Life and Relations, Volume III - by M.K. Gandhi
Plato Republic - A new translation by Robin Waterfield
Democracy in America - by Alexis de Tocqueville
Abraham Lincoln, Theologian of American Anguish - by Elton Trueblood
Black Mondays, Worst Decisions of the Supreme Court – by Joel D. Joseph
The Best Congress Money Can Buy – by Philip M. Stern
All you need to know about Ethics and Finance – Avinash D. Persaud and John Plender
Defying Corporations, Defining Democracy – edited by Dean Ritz
ON the Rampage, Corporate Predators and the Destruction of Democracy – by Russell Mokhiber and Robert Weissman
Free Elections ??? – by Howard Greenebaum
Winners and Losers – by Senator Paul Simon
The Best Democracy Money Can Buy – by Greg Palast
10 Steps to Repair American Democracy – by Steven Hill
The Buying of the President – by Charles Lewis and the Center for Public Integrity
America Robbed Blind – by Greg Farrell, investigative reporter USA TODAY
Breach of Trust – by Dr. Tom A. Coburn, former U.S. Congressman and John Hart
End Legalized Bribery – Cecil Heftel, former US Congressman

Honest Graft – Brooks Jackson

How Democratic Is America? – essays by Walter Berns, Howard Zinn, Sidney Hook, Harry M. Clor, and Allan Bloom

Save Your Job, Save Our Country – by Ross Perot and Pat Choate

Pigs at the Trough – by Arianna Huffington

Power and Money – by Thomas Byrne Edsall

Democracy Under Pressure – by Milton C. Cummings, Jr. and David Wise

Our America – by LeAlan Jones and Lloyd Newman

Labor Pains – by Suzan Erem

Myths of Free Trade – by Congressman Sherrod Brown

Naming the System, Inequality and Work in the Global Economy – by Michael D. Yates

The Three Trillion War – by Joseph E. Stiglitz (winner of Nobel Prize-Economics) and Linda J. Bilmes(former assistant secretary and chief financial officer of US Department of Commerce)

FreeFall – by Joseph E. Stiglitz

The Return of Depression Economics – by Paul Krugman (winner of Nobel Prize-Economics)

COLLAPSE – by Jared Diamond (winner of Pulitzer Prize)

The Great Depression of 1990 – by Dr. Ravi Batra

War is A Racket – by US Marine General Smedley D. Butler

Maverick Marine General Smedley D. Butler- by Hans Schmidt

The Phoenix Program – by Douglas Valentine

The Advisor, The Phoenix Program in Vietnam – by Lt. Colonel John L. Cook

WHITEOUT, The CIA, Drugs and the Press- by Alexander Cockburn and Jeffrey St. Clair

Against All Enemies _ by Richard Clarke (former National Coordinator for Security, Infrastructure Protection, and Counterterrorism under Presidents Clinton and George W. Bush)

Armed Madhouse – by Greg Palast

The Fall of the Shah – Fereydoun Hoveyda

All the Shah's Men, An American Coup and the roots of Middle East terror – by Stephen Kinzer

The Pinochet File, A declassified dossier on atrocity and accountability – by Peter Kornbluh

Rogue State – by William Blum

Imperial Democracy – by Ernest R. May

The Bases of Empire, the global struggle against U.S. military posts- edited by Catherine Lutz

9-11 - by Noam Chomsky

The Speech, and Its Context, Jacob Blaustein's Speech, "the meaning of Palestine Partition to American Jews" (Feb. 15, 1948) – by Abba A. Solomon

Live from Palestine _ edited by Nancy Stohlman and Laurieann Aladin

The Forever War – by Dexter Filkins (foreign correspondent for NY Times, former finalist for Pulitzer Prize and winner of George Polk Award)

The Enigma of Japanese Power – by Karel van Wolferen

The Japan that can say no – by Shintaro Ishihara

AGENTS OF INFLUENCE, How Japan's lobbyists in the United States manipulate America's political and economic system – by Pat Choate

HEAD TO HEAD, the coming economic battle among Japan, Europe, and America – by Lester Thurow

And the horse he rode in on – by James Carville

Brown – by Orville Schell

There's nothing in the middle of the road but yellow stripes and dead armadillos – by Jim Hightower

Locked in the cabinet - by Robert R. Reich

Stupid White Men – by Michael Moore

The Great Limbaugh Con, and other right-wing assaults on common sense – by Charles M. Kelly

Dick, the man who is President – by John Nichols

Hard Right, the rise of Jesse Helms – by Ernest B. Furgurson

The Problem of the Media, US communication politics in the 21st century – by Robert W. McChesney

Rich Media, Poor Democracy – by Robert W. McChesney

Tragedy & Farce, how the American Media sell Wars, Spin Elections, and Destroy Democracy – by John Nichols and Robert W. McChesney

The Exception to the RULERS, exposing oily politicians, war profiteers, and the Media that love them – by Amy Goodman with David Goodman

The Super Pollsters, how they measure and manipulate public opinion in America – by David W. Moore

Pesticide Alert – by Lawrie Mott & Karen Snyder (Natural Resources Defense Council)

Vital Signs 1997 – Lester R. Brown, Michael Renner, and Christopher Flavin WorldWatch Institute

Plan B 2.0, Rescuing a Planet under stress and a civilization in trouble – by Lester R. Brown

The Riverkeepers, Two activists fight to reclaim our environment as a basic human right – by John Cronin and Robert F. Kennedy, Jr.

The Last Well Person, How to stay well despite the health–care system _ by Nortin M. Hadler M.D.

Appetite for Profit, how the food industry undermines our health and how to fight back – by Michele Simon

Worst Pills Best Pills, a consumer's guide to avoiding drug-induced death or illness – by Sidney M. Wolfe, M.D., Larry D. Sasich, Pharm. D, M.P.H., Peter Lurie, M.D. , M.P.H. and Public Citizen's Health Research Group

The China Study, the most comprehensive study of nutrition ever conducted – by T. Colin Campbell, PhD and Thomas M. Campbell II
Prevent and Reverse Heart Disease, the revolutionary, scientifically proven nutrition-based cure – by Caldwell B. Esselstyne, Jr., M.D.

ABOUT THE AUTHOR

HOWARD M GREENEBAUM grew up in Baltimore, Maryland, USA, and survived some serious illnesses, including polio, pneumonia, and asthma. From the beginning, he learned to be a survivor, and never looked back on past difficulties. He excelled in sports, and won many awards in swimming races. After attending Duke University and Ohio State University, he joined his father in their diversified international enterprises. He achieved a US patent on a security system that he marketed internationally. His different business interests required him to travel around the world. With all of his involvement in commerce, he still found time to coach high school basketball teams for over 30 years. In 1984 he won the Democratic nomination for the US Congress in Maryland. In 1988 he won the Democratic nomination for the US Congress in California. Both times he lost in the General Elections to heavily financed Republican incumbents. After the 1988 election loss, he wrote his first book entitled, "Free Elections???" On the book cover was an American flag with a hole in it, and $100 bills flowing through it. At the age of 82, Howard has retained the same enthusiasm for advocacy for better government. This book is a great contribution for citizens all over the world to learn how to achieve clean governance. Howard has been quoted many times for his slogan, "We will never get a clean environment with a dirty government!"